Towers, Temples, Palaces

Ryan Frawley

Table of Contents

Our revels now are ended. These our actors,

As I foretold you, were all spirits, and

Are melted into air, into thin air:

And like the baseless fabric of this vision,

The cloud-capp'd tow'rs, the gorgeous palaces,

The solemn temples, the great globe itself,

Yea, all which it inherit, shall dissolve,

And, like this insubstantial pageant faded,

Leave not a rack behind.

- The Tempest, Act 4 Scene 1

Never Home

Blame it on Brexit. I never thought the vote would go the way it did, and that the country I was born in would decide to tear itself away from the rest of Europe. I thought I'd always be an EU citizen, with the right to live and work anywhere I chose in twenty-eight different countries. And because I always had the right, I never used it. It was only the thought I might lose a life I had always dreamed of but never pursued that made us take the leap we did.

In a small park overlooking the mountain-encircled port of Vancouver, we searched for holiday rentals on A's phone. Perhaps we never would have married if not to make her an EU citizen, too. We'd been together for more than ten years without feeling any need to make it legal. But there are times when the craziest ideas start to make sense. I had just started a new job, but she could work from anywhere. And my writing paid a modest sum every month. Intending to stay in Vancouver, we'd just poured money into renovating our apartment. Deciding to blow it all off and travel around Europe for an indefinite period was wildly out of character for two planners like us. But that's what we did. Starting in Italy, we stayed for six months before moving to southern France for a year, then back to Italy.

And the wildest ideas are sometimes the best you'll ever have.

A hundred years ago, ancient empires crumbled and collapsed for less than this. A home. A homeland. A place of one's own. A sense of belonging, of standing still on one particular and favored rock while an ocean of white-capped time surges all around.

This means nothing to me.

Maybe it's in my blood. For generations, my ancestors farmed the same wild corner of Ireland, clinging to the barren rock through famine and hardship. But the world changed, and war came, and my grandfather left his home as a young man and never came back. My father lives now in the city he was born in, but he spent his adult life wandering the world, across continents and hemispheres, the miles behind him fading away like the white plume of a passenger jet carving its way across a friendly sky. They say that the red in my beard, the parts that were the first to turn white, is a Scandinavian trait. (There were no such thing as Vikings, I've read. There were simply men who went Viking, following the sea road to richer lands. A verb, not a noun.) This could go back a long way.

I don't have a home, really. I'm not homeless in the sense that the word has come to mean, though. I pay the rent with writing (so like and share and tell your friends to do the same, please!). In the last couple of years, we - me and my wife and our cat - haven't spent more than six months in one spot. We don't have to live like this. We like it.

My lifestyle isn't anyone's concern besides my own, of course. But I see this everywhere. Especially in Canada, especially in America, in England, in France. No one is from here. And in the swollen cities of this century, no one can afford to stay for long. You grab on and hold on, in a city like Vancouver, or San Francisco, or London or Paris or New York, for as long as you can. And every year the rent goes up, and every year your money gets stretched a little more, a wild and raving heretic on a medieval rack, until one day it's over. Your grip slips and away you go, flung by centripetal force out to the suburbs and their dreary commutes. Or to another city, another country.

Meanwhile, if you're one of the lucky ones, maybe you'll actually buy a home the way our parents did. So now you're renting from the bank instead. Besides, homes aren't places to live. Didn't you get the memo? They're investments, brick-and-mortar machines that turn bullshit into money while you watch fake numbers rise on paper and pay real cash in ever-growing taxes on theoretical future gains. Houses are no longer homes. They're rungs on an endless ladder, more escalator than staircase. And you're running desperately up the down side for as long as you can.

Maybe the snails and the crabs have it right. Maybe the only real home you'll ever know is the one you carry with you. The space you take up, casting your tiny shadow against the bright immensity all around. I like that. I like the thought that for as long as my heart keeps knocking in my ribs, I'll always be home. And after that, who knows? Maybe we merge again with the stars we came from, our atoms re-fusing with the cosmos we've fooled ourselves into thinking we're separate from.

Until then, I'll be right here.

First Night In Formia

It was our first night in Formia, the Italian coastal town that became our first home in Europe. After another in a long line of sleepless nights and eye-stingingly early mornings, A's afternoon nap went into overtime. The cat slept too, curled up in the crook of A's knees, shielding her eyes with her asymmetrical feet.

Through the open window, I could hear the sea breathing, as though it, too, was asleep. And I alone was awake, in an unfamiliar town with nothing in the house to drink. Pulling the peeling front door of our new home shut behind me, I went for a walk.

The Gulf of Gaeta glittered. Emperors used to vacation here. The ruins of the villa belonging to Tiberius were discovered in the 50s, just up the coast in Sperlonga. And now we live here.

The corner store was closed, as I knew it would be on Sunday evening. Outside the pizzeria, a crowd fragmented. A wedding in Formia, the warm night air bright with confetti and staccato Italian. I walked on.

The sorceress Circe could turn men into pigs - though some might argue that's not such a difficult trick to pull off. Lions and wolves roamed around her house. When Ulysses and his men arrived, she drugged them and transformed them into animals. Ulysses, spared by divine intervention, drew his sword and threatened the witch, freeing his men and becoming her lover. For one year, the mythic wanderer stayed with Circe on the mountain that bears her name, overlooking the Tyrrhenian sea near Formia.

Along the beach, the street pulsed with life. Old couples walking silently together like pair-bonded birds. Families taking their children to the playground near the beach. Teenagers smoking in bored-looking packs. Everyone was out, lit by streetlights against the black sea. You'd never see that in Canada, where nights belong only to the young and the destitute. Respectable people stay home in front of their screens.

I followed Via Tito Scipione along the shore, drifting like a ghost through the locals. This, if I'm honest, is me at my most comfortable. In a tower. On a boat. At the top of a mountain. Observing but remote.

There was some event at the harbor, right beside the villa that once belonged to Cicero. A huge white tent, glowing in the dark night air. There was a bar inside. I could see the ubiquitous red and white Peroni beer company logo through the open entrance. But I wasn't invited.

The boats jostled one another gently, the soft slap of the water against their sides like a kiss. Flies swarmed in clusters around the streetlights, and bats swooped silently in and out of the darkness to snatch a meal. I watched a fat yellow moon rise slowly above the sleeping ships, distorted by heat and warm air to look twice the size it should.

The first time I moved to a foreign country, I used to look at the sky a lot. Everything was different. The weather, the food, the customs. The accent, though not the language. I was alone, 6000 kilometers from home, not knowing where to go or how to live or what the future would hold. But the stars were the same, the same stars that still shine in my father's garden, showing over the crumbling century-old buildings of Hastings Street, sparkling in the broken glass and shining on the dulled points of discarded needles. It was comforting, even though I knew my night was day for everyone back home. The same stars. The same moon with its haunted mournful face. The same swirling sky. It would surprise me sometimes, swinging into view between the buildings on either side of a vacant lot. Outshining the crown of floodlights on the brow of Grouse Mountain.

I turned for home, our new home. Walking back along the shore, I watched over my shoulder to make sure the moon was following. Like a faithful dog, it came with me, pushing a band of golden light across the bay in front of it as I led it home to show to A. Silently it rose behind me, climbing over the rooftops, high enough to be seen from our south facing balcony as I unlocked the iron gate in front of the apartment building.

Inside, A was still sleeping. I took up a pen. Insulted, the moon went on its lonely way.

Rome Alone

No one finds themselves. That's not why we travel. You're right there, where you always were. But sometimes a foreign sun can show you to yourself in a different light, the veins of quartz that shine in the flashlight's blue beam as we make our way through the cave. To see yourself through the eyes of a stranger, even for half a second, is to confront an enigma.

I was buzzing, floating two inches off the floor as I climbed down the metal stairs hastily rolled up to the side of the plane. Rome has never been my home, but I've been fortunate enough to occasionally feel as though it is. After a few happy days in the gray grandeur of Vienna, the Italian sun wrapped its arms around me, and I beamed back at her while my blood swarmed.

At the time, we were living in Formia, a coastal town ninety minutes from Rome on the cheap train. My wife, our new marriage pasted on top of an old relationship like a FRAGILE sticker on a mistreated suitcase, was waiting for me there. She'd left Vienna a day before I had, to allow me time to do some research she had no interest in. Besides, we have a cat to consider. But I never miss a chance to spend time in Rome. There was no reason for me to rush home. I took the slow train from the airport to Termini and stepped out into the long-shadowed chaos of my favorite city on earth.

I was eighteen when I first came to Rome. I was alone then, too. This was before the Euro, before the World Trade Center fell, before soldiers patrolled the streets of every capital in Europe, arms draped over downwards-pointed rifles. This was before I dropped out of university, before I stopped believing in the inherited myths I'd been raised with. I don't believe that the world was any brighter then than it is now, but memory makes it look that way. No city on earth demonstrates the way the past can be made to shine the way that Rome does. It can be seductive, the past. But it only loves you once you're gone.

After 2001, I moved across the world, and it was 2014 before I found my way back to the Eternal City. I'd thought then, with the woman who was to become my wife at my side, that there was no way that Rome could measure up to my memories of it. But if anything, I found myself falling more deeply in love with the place than ever before. And so, in 2016, when she and I decided to change our lives and move to Europe, it was Italy we moved to first.

So I've seen the sights. The churches. The museums. The Coliseum's vast bulk, crouching in its pit at the side of the straight highway Mussolini had built at enormous cost to the irreplaceable ruins below. As beautiful as Rome's attractions are, I don't go for that. Instead, I made my way down Via Cavour, grabbing a couple of heavy bottles of beer from a corner store as I made my way to the steps near the wedding-cake-shaped monument to Italy's first king. I'm not going to plead for authenticity here. For a foreigner, especially one who doesn't speak Italian, il vero Italia remains out of reach. I don't go to Rome to see Italians, or not only them, anyway. The entire world descends on this city, day after day, the airports and train stations disgorging blinking crowds in every costume and every language of the globe. In Rome, I sit in the light and watch the whole world parade past.

The sun moved slowly across the stone steps, where budget-minded tourists bring a sandwich for a break from the city's inflated prices. I fished a battered notebook out of my backpack, a silver pen tucked into the wire spiral of its spine. Vienna's gilded hallways still echoed inside me, the breakthrough I'd made in the novel I was writing in a budget hotel with a view of the Riesenrad still filling me with borrowed - ok, stolen -

light. Creativity begets inspiration, and not the other way around, as many people think. Surrounded by the buzz of a hundred different languages, my own words spilled out across the page in the lazy Roman sun, the stones ringing with the buzz of the centuries as I turned brown alcohol into purple prose.

And that's when it happened, those little moments of gilded magic that make up Rome, just as much as the pitted marble and shattered columns. The senseless splendour of the everyday, the sun-glutted throb of a wasp, the fine hairs that rise on our skin as the hand of a lover draws near. Looking up from the page to take another swig of Peroni, I saw a family passing close in front of me. Mother, father, son, all with that harried look of tourists in Rome for the first time, overwhelmed by traffic and heat and relentless street hustlers trying to sell selfie sticks and friendship bracelets. Not the daughter, though. She was looking right at me. And she was smiling as though she had never seen anything quite like me.

I've never been good at guessing people's ages, but I'd put her at around twelve. Young enough that her eyes still shone, before we see enough and fear enough to dim them. As she followed along in the wake of her scowling father and harassed mother, she turned her head to keep her eyes on me. I never heard a word from any of them, and couldn't even guess where they had come from. But wherever she called home, I imagined that she had never seen someone sitting out in public, writing by hand. I imagine her as a writer herself, young enough to believe that something so ludicrous could be an actual career path, just like I did at her age. I imagine her remembering that, seeing an adult writing for no reason beyond their own pleasure, and being encouraged to keep making her own art. Within a few steps, she and her family were swallowed up in the swirling crowd. For her, foreigner that I am, I was part of the scenery of Rome, part of the same fascination that gripped me when I first saw the city and has never let me go since.

Rome gives you these moments constantly. There's always another door opening to show you something you've never seen before in a square you thought was utterly familiar. The light is forever changing, even though the sun is the same one that baked the dusty streets when the Caesars rode in triumph through marble arches. It's unbelievably ancient, and it's always new. Every time I step off a train, I half expect to meet myself, eighteen, troubled, hungry, and confused. But I wouldn't smile at myself the way that young girl did. By the time I found Rome, I thought I was past that kind of light-heartedness. I thought I knew how the world worked, and I didn't like it. Rome showed me then what it continues to remind me now. Emperor, Pope, priest or peasant, we each contain our own stories, an ancient city in miniature, visible only in the briefest glimpses to those who keep their eyes open.

When a conquering Emperor rode his chariot through the streets in honor of some military victory, a single slave stood beside him and whispered in his ear: Remember, you are just a man. In Rome, you can still hear the whispered words bouncing back from the worn marble of toppled temples. But it was the hands of men that built Rome. Who could want anything more?

The Miracle of the Everyday

I'm not superstitious. I don't believe in signs and omens. As though the future can be seen somehow in steaming entrails or the filth at the bottom of a cup. Nonsense. The universe is not a novelist, and it doesn't foreshadow. Making stories is a human concern, not a cosmic one.

But I do believe in magic.

I always take the window seat, and not just because I'm a huge fan of personal space. As the plane rolled slowly to the runway, I read a mediocre book and waited. But when those big engines start to roar, the book goes down. There's that sky again, paler and calmer than the sea that runs white fingers along the grassy edge of the runway itself. I crane my neck to peer through the awkwardly offset spiracle of the triple-paned window. And the plane begins to move, and the white painted lines on the runway streak past, faster and faster, chasing one another into the past, and the wings tremble in the suddenly raging air, and the sea and the runway fall away together as the plane lumbers into the sky.

These are the moments that approach something of the religious for me. If I had a hat, I might be inclined to take it off. The plane at a forty-five-degree angle, half angel, half leviathan, its nose already in the air while its back wheels still race along the ground. It's awe. It's a miracle, no matter how many times a day it happens. This unimaginable weight of people and suitcases and metal and fuel springing into the air as though born for the sky.

But the miracle passes us by, worn with overuse. Once, I flew from Edmonton to Vancouver on a bright, clear day, and the endless beauty of the Rocky Mountains below was matched only by wonder at the passenger's disinterest. Window shades drop; all that high-altitude sunlight makes it hard to play games on your phone. We don't need mountains; we have pictures of them. They look better with an Instagram filter anyway, don't they?

I'm not saying I'm any better. We need to ignore the miracles that are occurring every day, all around us. If we didn't, we wouldn't be here at all. Those of our ancestors who could spend an entire day in rapt wonder at the green of the trees ended up as wolf dung. The callous brutes survived, and prospered, and gave birth to us. Flying is one of the only times when I'm unable to ignore it, that's all. A mundane thing I've never gotten used to, no matter how many times I see it.

Forfeit awe, and the universe becomes a marketplace. Unfortunately for us, though, the beauty and the wonder is heavily top-loaded. They don't bring the bill until you've already had the meal. And we get old and tired, and our eyes thicken with the years, and we forget what children know. When I think of all the hospital vigils I probably have coming my way, the losses that will inevitably mount up, the horrible price of absence that is the inevitable cost of caring for anyone in this world, I dread the waiter approaching with that bill. It all has to be paid for, you know. The joy, the beauty, the rapture. It comes at a price. And this is not a European restaurant, either, where they'll let you sit at your table all night without bothering you. The service here is American-style. The bill comes when it comes, not when you're ready for it. If you're ever ready for it.

The only way I've found so far to stave off the fear of that bill is to try to live in such a way that when it does come, it will have been worth it. It's coming anyway. But if the feast is everything you hoped - well then, who cares what it cost? Hence the flights, the travel, the hunger for the bright places of the world. The sparrow that launches itself into the wide open sky.

A Tourist in the Trenches

I reached Kobarid - Caporetto in Italian - almost a hundred years to the day after the battle. It's beautiful country. Tall mountains rise on either side of the bright blue waters of the Soca river, which the Italians call the Isonzo. A perfect autumn day, bright and warm, the leaves glowing gold as they fell, dry and rattling, from the trees. On a lonely mountain road, I stopped my rented car to watch the sun gild the mountains as it guttered like a failing candle into twilight. Across the fields, the chiming of cowbells drifted through the still air. The herds were heading home. The white spire of the village church caught the last of the light before the white-veined mountains cut it off.

Molto bella, no? One more picture to store on my hard drive. But for some men, it was the last thing they ever saw.

*

War tourism. Doesn't sound right, does it? It doesn't always feel right, either. But I'm interested in history, and much of human history is very, very dark. In fact - and this may be a flaw in our species, or maybe it's a flaw in me - the darkest chapters are often the most interesting.

The First World War is difficult. No longer within living memory, it remains far less understood than the Second. It's further from us in time, a relic of a different world. And while it had its share of fascinating personalities, they hardly compare to the likes of Hitler, Churchill, Stalin, and FDR. But most of all, the First World War is less popular today because it lacks the clear moral lines of the Second. World War Two was one of the rare occasions where real life had good guys and bad guys. And even rarer, the bad guys lost. Admittedly, it would be a stretch to call the Allies genuinely good, but there's no doubt that Nazism was a great evil. Compared to Hitler, even a monster like Stalin comes off looking good.

World War One is not so easy. Kaiser Wilhelm may have been a pompous and belligerent ass, but so were most other monarchs of his day. Britain fought not to protect neutral Belgium, but to preserve its naval supremacy, so crucial to its international empire. Russia was a corrupt and horribly unequal society, rotten to its core. But Tsar Nicholas cuts a tragic figure in light of what happened to him and the family he doted on. And the American involvement, at a stage when the conflict was so far advanced, can seem more motivated by opportunism than any moral convictions.

Even by the standards of World War One, the Italian Front is often forgotten. The overriding image of the war - for English speakers, at least - is the mud and blood of trench warfare, in Flanders, at Ypres and the Somme, at Passchendaele, at Verdun. We hear far less about the conflict between Italy and Austria-Hungary in the mountains along their borders. Everything that makes the First World War less popular than the second goes double here. On one side, we have the crumbling Hapsburg empire that started the war and then fought it so ineptly. On the other, we have the new nation of Italy, bound by treaty to help Germany and Austria, yet taking up arms against them for purely cynical reasons. It's not easy to pick a side here, if you're the type that needs to do that. But it's a fascinating chapter of history, for exactly that reason. There's no easy peg on which to hang your moral judgments. Every man who fought on the Italian Front was fighting for a lost cause, no matter what side he was on. Austria-Hungary didn't survive the war, but Italy achieved almost none of its aims, either, and instead began the slide into fascism. The Italian Front is messy. No good guys. No bad guys either. No winners, only losers. It's the entire war in miniature.

*

Outside of Kobarid, the scars are still there. In the woods at Ravelnik, you can wander through the preserved trenches and into a long cave carved into the hill by Hapsburg troops, and you'll be entirely alone, except for the dead. A metal detector here could still find ammunition cartridges and shell fragments in the undergrowth just off the narrow trail that winds through the trees. A shovel would turn up foreign bones.

There are more trenches high on the hills at Kolovrat. Here, the trees are few and far between, struggling for thin air on the rocky slopes. A hundred years ago, no trees grew so high. Today's Italian - Slovenian border runs right along the lines of these trenches, marked only by a low concrete pillar. Industrialized slaughter on a massive scale, for what? Lines on a map, and a border you can now wander across at will.

It isn't fun, touring these places, despite the natural beauty of this part of Slovenia. It's sobering. It's upsetting, sometimes. It's fascinating. The sacrifices made by these strangers meant something, even if their cause didn't. It's the purest luck that you were born in this time, and not theirs, in a country willing to throw away its youth on ignoble ends.

I don't really believe in progress. The medieval peasant was at least as intelligent as the modern wage-slave, and quite possibly more fulfilled. We've known the world was round for millennia, long before Columbus' voyage. The ancient Greeks had computers. The Babylonians used electricity. The past is a lie. Don't let them - the advertisers, the propagandists, the cynical cheerleaders of the current order - tell you that people a decade ago were mindless apes, beating one another with rocks over a flyblown antelope carcass. It's not true.

But in this, at least, we can claim some progress. War goes on. People are dying right now, for reasons as obscure as they are inadequate. But mechanized slaughter on the scale of that of the two World Wars is almost vanished from living memory. That can only be progress.

And now, birds sing over the trenches that still scar the mountains, and the occasional morbid-minded tourist picks his way over the broken ground. I know nothing of war. You could argue that it's voyeuristic, this interest of mine in the horrors of the past. Certainly, it's not how most would choose to spend their vacation, which is why A stayed at home for this trip. But it's important to remember. It's important to understand why the world is the way that it is, and how everything that looks so stable and solid can collapse so suddenly. Atrocity begins with ignorance. Don't forget. Don't look away. Or else you won't see it when it comes around again.

Sparrows

Sparrows live here.

It stays warm all year, of course, and the crumbs of overpriced food dropped by passing travelers who eat from boredom more than hunger are enough to raise a family on. I know that the birds live here, raising chicks in the steel rafters and shitting on the polished floor, rather than it being a case of a few unlucky individuals getting trapped and lost inside the cavernous space of the airport. Because I've seen them before. I've been here before. I almost live here myself.

We've all been here before. The droning chatter. The manufactured smells. The facsimile food. The silent, highly decorous and utterly ruthless war for power outlets. It doesn't need describing. One echoing departure hall mimics all the others. Even the languages hardly change. After so long abroad, my head turns by itself at the sound of English being spoken. At the airport, I hear it a lot.

It'll be English and French in Edmonton, too. My phone, set on top of the half-empty case at my side, chimes regularly with updates. An ocean and most of a continent away, my brother is killing time in a place just like this, waiting for his flight while I wait for mine.

The sparrows drop quickly from their perches above the shops, tiny wings blurred by motion as they fall. That's the look I was trying to achieve when I had a sparrow tattooed on my arm years ago. The memory's corners have become rounded from frequent replay. Damp air rising from towering trees and a faint mist hovering over the dark water of the lake. My footsteps hollow on the small wooden bridge. The cloud of twittering sparrows bursting from the bushes and surrounding me in an instant. I can still feel one bird's twiggy toes on my outstretched finger while the bright black bead of its eye stared into mine.

I'm not superstitious. The universe doesn't drop hints, and the birds know no more than we do. But when I heard that my grandmother had died, was dying in England while the Canadian sparrows swarmed around me, it felt like something. Sparrows used to be seen as psychopomps, creatures that carry the souls of the dead to the next life. The tattoo came later.

All of this happened in a different world. Before smartphones, before messenger apps. Back then, my brother lived in England, and I lived in Canada. Now he lives in Canada, and I live nowhere. Like an airport sparrow, I find what warmth I can and call it home.

I could say that what I'm doing now is going home, but it doesn't feel like it. England hasn't been home to me since long before I left. Even if every time I go back to my dad's house, it feels in some ways as though I never left. As though all those years, the airports, the jobs, the girls, the triumphs and setbacks were just the fleeting dreams of a frustrated loser. At least there's no tragedy this time. The last time both my brother and I were under our father's roof, it was for a funeral. But there's no loss this time to draw us back upstream. It's a vacation.

My phone has fallen silent. He's in the air now, en route to Toronto, to Frankfurt, to Birmingham. I'll beat him there by a full twelve hours or more. Even the miracle of human flight has its limits.

It's always warm in the airport, even in the winter. Even in the freakish snow that fell in the French Riviera yesterday, while a storm named Emma gripped England in her teeth. But today, the Mediterranean sun is slanting through the windows, casting hot rectangles of light on the polished floor and making the fallen crumbs of food look twice as large, twinned by their shadows. The sparrows have their food, their shelter, their nests tucked into inaccessible corners of the high ceiling where the maintenance staff don't go. But do they ever miss the wide blue sky that shines outside, just on the far side of a pane of glass?

It was the very first time that I flew out of Nice, when I stood in the unmoving line in the jetway, waiting to get onto a plane. The sun was cooking us slowly as we waited. Fellow passengers fanned themselves with paper tickets. Outside the hot glass, on a small metal platform, a dead bird lay with its tiny legs curled up into the air. Mistaking the view through the window for the open sky, it had flown joyfully at the pane and broken its neck. But no cage held it; no predator tore it apart. It died with that bright blue sky in its eyes.

The Wasteland: Leonard Cohen Is Dead

On the day Leonard Cohen died, I was on a train to Naples. It was late. I watched the rain fall in soft sheets from the roof over the dripping platform, the logo of the cement works on the concrete sleepers filling up with rain between the glistening rails. The train was ancient, and half a kilometre long. Hoisting my soggy bag onto the overhead rack, I slumped in my seat, put on some headphones and watched the parade of distant towns I'll never visit rise out of the mist and sink back, one by one, into a fold of the mountains. My legs ached. We had spent the day before wandering the silent ruins of Minturno, where the old temples are abandoned, the stone road smoothed by the centuries but still bearing the wheel ruts of the chariots that used to race from here to Rome. With every year that passes, we feel our bodies more and our souls less. The rivers slow and deposit their silt in our veins, and what used to be a raging torrent becomes a muddy estuary.

It makes you feel. That's what art does. It doesn't need to be more complicated than that. It dredges the river. When I was a gloomy teenager, sadness seemed like a virtue, and misery was a mask I wore between myself and the world that called me by name. The sky was the colour of my eyes. The streets formed a map of my bright red veins. But I grew into the shape of a man, armed and armoured, a man the world didn't recognize. I left. And the space I left behind will stay empty forever.

This is how you enter the Wasteland, one grey day after another. It's haunted me since the moment the bright constellation of childhood began to fall from my eyes. When the world doesn't talk to you, and you don't talk to it. But I was lucky. The sad songs led me past sadness. Each knight enters the forest alone, by a path laid out just for them. It was there before they were born.

The Wasteland flourished again when its king was healed, restored by the weapon that wounded him. Beauty has haunted me, ever since I was old and ugly enough to recognize it. That shattering moment, that blissful annihilation I swayed beneath, a sapling under the storm, as I gazed at Michelangelo's Pieta, or read Lolita, or listened to Suzanne. I've never once in my life been alone, unless I've forgotten these things. The secret chart to get to the heart of the matter. The path through the forest.

"Even though it all went wrong,

I'll stand before the Lord of Song

With nothing on my tongue but Hallelujah."

The train danced on shimmering rails into the brightening morning, and I remembered something I once heard about eternity: that it has nothing to do with time. Any god worth the name must stand outside of time. If you or I or anyone is ever to meet it, we already have. The Eternal exists now. Or never.

There is a direct line between then and now. Some silver thread that spans distance as easily as time, that runs from the angry boy staring at the snow through the grimy windows of a shed to the entrepreneur taking a minute to listen to Suzanne on his smartphone under the bright sun of Hydra's harbour to me, now, hunching over a makeshift desk while the windows bleed condensation and the Tyrrhenian sea crashes outside.

We care about art in the same way we care about the poor: because we feel we should. Four-hour lines at the Uffizi Gallery, and how many of these people went to their hometown's art gallery this year? This is not an argument for snobbery. It's the opposite. Art is everyone's business. It belongs to us all.

Either it grabs you, or it doesn't. This is what I tell myself. And me and A, we pretend that this is just the way I am, some hobby of mine, the way Sunday football is sacred to millions of men. But that's not what this is, not exactly. This is darker than that. This is incense and blood. This is chanting from the darkness, the bellowing bull and the flashing blade, a throwback to a savagery 10,000 years of civilization have tried to protect her from. In lightless caves before history, men painted a world on the dripping walls. No one risks life and limb for a hobby. This is more akin to religion, crying Allahu Akbar as my jacket explodes. But where religion divides, art unites. Michelangelo's Pieta might belong to the Catholic Church, but they don't own it. The Louvre only holds the Mona Lisa; they can't contain it. Now more than ever, art is ethereal, non-corporeal, fragmented into megabytes and blasted into the digital ether.

Either it gets you, or it doesn't. I've been haunted by beauty, pursued by it the way God bothered all those marble-skinned saints. But if it ever stopped, I'd turn right around and start chasing it. Bach, when he wrote the Cello Suites, was considered a skilled tradesman, qualitatively no different from the guy who laid the floors in the salons he played. Now things have come full circle. There is no art, there is only entertainment. Songs are meant to be heard, not listened to. We don't have films, we only have movies. Every book is a series, every series a movie, every movie a cinematic universe devoted to selling merchandise.

It's sad when an artist passes, because there is no one to replace them. I've never been the type to bewail the present and paint the past in pastel colours. Previous generations had more than their share of forgettable dreck too. But I can't imagine what will last from these flimsy decades. Innovation has been abandoned for prolificity. Profundity runs shrieking from marketability. No one wants to listen, they just want to dance. Or worse. They want a beat to chop vegetables to.

I used to think that all this mattered, and then I decided it didn't. People can live however they want, and it's not for me or anyone else to decide what others should like. But like all healthy impulses, this one can go too far. Until you find yourself denying the truth, pretending that there is no such thing as quality and that the squawk of an autotuned Disney idol is the same as the skilled expression of a master. It's not. Quality exists, and it matters. Because art, real art, is not an adornment to life, much less an entertaining distraction. It is life. In and of itself. A great painting, a great song or a great novel does not reflect the world. It is the world, a world all of its own. And those songs will follow you forever, woven into your dreams, harder to forget than the faces of the dead you once loved.

The gloomy little 15-year-old who found solace for the disappointments of his working-class life in the songs of a Jewish Canadian poet is still here, somewhere. And the songs are still here too, raising the hairs on the back of my neck now just like they did then, though every cell of my body has changed. A wave crosses the entire world, even if the water doesn't. And a sliver of the same eternity hangs on the point of my pen.

When an artist dies, it matters. Because like Damascus steel, like Greek fire, we've forgotten how to make them.

Lyon

The train from Antibes to Marseilles takes less than half the time the bus needs. But it costs twice as much. During the time we spent in Juan les Pins, summer playground of the staggeringly wealthy, we were at our poorest. It was the bus for us. Two buses, in fact, from Juan to Cannes and then from Cannes to Marseilles. From there, a train carried us up from the coast, flakes of snow streaking like falling stars past the windows, as we rode to Lyon.

Lyon, I've since learned, is one of the world's great food cities. The home of French gastronomy. We wouldn't know. As vegetarians, the restaurants in France were almost universally closed to us. The French don't go in for vegetarianism as a rule. Even the salads drip with duck fat and pig juice.

So we ate Indian food and rode the funicular railway up the hill. Lyon, on the confluence of the Rhone and Saone rivers, has always been a crossroads. The meeting point of northern and southern Europe, where the order and productivity of the North merge with the exuberant joie de vivre of the South. The Romans were here, of course, building stony streets and digging out the hillside to make a theater. The streets are still there two thousand years later, and the theater is still in use. Though not in January. The snow of the highlands had melted into a gray drizzle, and we wandered through the ruined Roman town completely alone.

On the same hill the Romans colonized, a great gold Madonna stares down pitifully at the town from atop the Basilica of Notre Dame. The dazzling white church commemorates one of those miracles that seem to have died out in the Internet age. In 1643, when the plague was sweeping Europe, Lyon was saved by, reputedly, the intervention of the Virgin Mary. Each year on 8 December, faithful Lyonnaise would place lit candles in their windows to thank the Virgin for saving them. From this tradition grew the Fete des Lumieres, an event which now draws tourists from all over the world to see the city lit up in an extravagant electrical display.

I didn't want to go to Lyon. It's not that I emphatically didn't want to go. It just wasn't a city I knew a lot about. Despite the Joseph Roth essays I read about the place, nothing specific made me dream of Lyon. But like everywhere I've been in France, Lyon's charm is slow and pernicious. Though it was once Roman, Lyon was never Rome. It doesn't bowl you over with soaring monuments and ruined magnificence. Instead, it lulls you, so calmly and confidently that you barely notice it happening. Unlocked doors creak open at a push to reveal medieval courtyards and tunnels for you to wander at will. In the square in front of the Cathedral, the Place Saint-Jean, booksellers set up stalls under the watchful eye of Mother Mary. Wander the cobbled streets and squares that were lively even in January, and drop by drop, your heart fills up.

They would ban the squares if they could, you know. Younger, less enlightened jurisdictions already have. The glass-eyed cities of Canada, of America, rarely have a public square that belongs to everyone. Revolutions ferment in such places. Mobs bloom. Slogans are chanted, and royal heads roll. The town square is a dangerous place for the powerful. No wonder they're banished from modern cities. But in France and all across Europe, the hearts of the cities are open to the sky. Especially in the sunny South, where people live their lives in the square, in full view of their neighbors and the proud sun.

To be clear, Lyon gets its share of tourists. But unlike Paris, it's not overwhelmed by them. It's still French that you hear in the squares and on the streets. And the notorious French rudeness - far rarer even in Paris than reputation would have you believe - is absent here. No one goes to Lyon in January. And every shopkeeper and stall holder and restaurant owner seemed happy to see us. Happy to share the charm of their underrated town. Lyon is an old city, but it doesn't feel that way. Its venerable age has made it joyful and bright instead of gray and dour.

We didn't have long in Lyon. While A braved a deli to get some sandwiches for the train ride back, I bought a plastic cup of *vin chaud* from a table set up on the other side of the street. And as steam curled from my hand and boozy warmth spread through my chest, I was glad we had come to Lyon. There were no adventures, and no wild stories to tell. Instead, there was just the flirtatious charm of a great French city, smiling shyly even in the rain and beckoning us to return someday.

Quillan: Evening in the Garden

There is no geographical solution to an emotional problem. Tony Soprano said that. But he's not the only one. There is no shortage of shark-hearted platitude peddlers ready to tell you that you can't escape your problems by leaving them, even as they offer you another pill. And like all truisms, it's sometimes true. A schizophrenic will still hallucinate in Helsinki or Helena. The malignant narcissist will poison Yonkers and Yekaterinburg equally.

But what they don't tell you is that the version of you that stands on a Paris pavement, overwhelmed by the sudden Stendahlian perfection of it all, is not the same person as you are now. The past is a story we tell ourselves over and over, no more real than the exploits of a TV mobster. Change your situation, and you change yourself.

Any immigrant knows this. But British people are never immigrants. We're only ever expats, with its decadent connotations of supper clubs and afternoon drinks and the fading glow of Empire.

We only found our way to the small town of Quillan, with its population of 3500 split between native French and Anglophone - mostly British – ex-pats by chance. We needed somewhere affordable to spend the summer, but close enough to major cities to allow us to catch flights when we wanted to. Close to the Spanish border, Quillan has hot, dry summers and is surrounded by mountains. Plus, the owner of the apartment we found – the upper floor of a house, actually – spoke fluent English.

In fact, she turned out to be a Londoner. As was the woman across the street, married to a Welshman. Next-door lived Scottish Derek and American Laura. A few houses up the hill, Pat and Sheila from Liverpool were also part of the social circle. Unwittingly, we had found ourselves in a bona fide ex-pat community.

No one moves to France to hang out with English people. But after six months of never having a conversation that wasn't with each other, even an introvert like me could see an upside to social interaction. And the gardens of Quillan are gorgeous on a summer evening, with the dogs napping and the stars starting to show in the purple sky that sings with the bells from the church. The people of Quillan, the ragtag group of foreigners that have made their home in an obscure town in the mountains, couldn't have been more welcoming.

The ex-pat is fundamentally different from the refugee. One chases a dream while the other flees a nightmare. And it's not a question of money. The history of the 20th century alone will give you plenty of tales of rich refugees. The ex-pats of Quillan have chased their dreams to wind up here, in the castle crowned bowl of the hills pierced by winding rivers, granite gorges, and precipitous balcony roads. The accents you hear on the drowsy tables in the garden after nightfall are mostly British, but you would never mistake Quillan for the rain-sodden country of my birth. In this community and thousands like it all across France and Spain and elsewhere in Europe, people live blessed lives of their own devising, halfway between past and perfect.

But they're not just going to let you sit in the sun and sip wine while the clouds sink down the flanks of the mountains. The world comes for us all, sooner or later. And if not for Brexit, maybe we never would have moved to Europe in the first place. It was only the threat of my British passport becoming worth less than it has been all my life that made us take our two-year journey around the EU. In Quillan and all the places like it, there is a fear, no matter what people tell themselves. A fear that, no matter

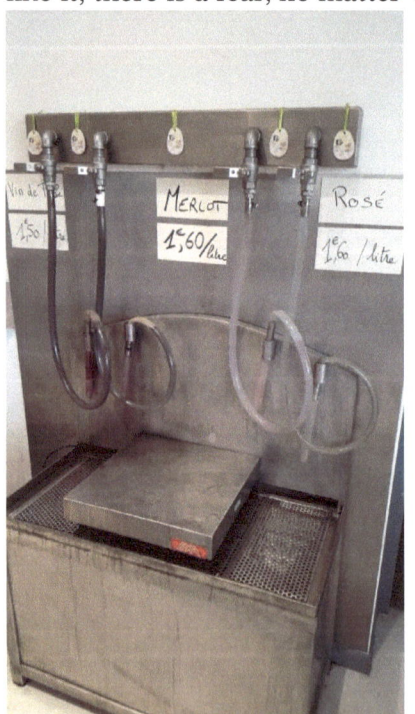

what they do, an ex-pat's right to remain in the home they have made for themselves could be suddenly taken away.

We all live in a vortex of uncertainty. All we know is that this can't last. The mountains will fall just as the trees do, only slower. Everything seeks its end. In a cave above the village of Ariege, the strange signs painted 15,000 years ago can still be seen today, but they won't last forever. Set against the life of mountains, we humans have barely a heartbeat's space to see what surrounds us before we vanish into the shadows at the far end of the cave.

But then, anyone familiar with French cooking knows that a single bite, if the food is rich enough, can be plenty. A single moment of life, any life, sliced any way you please, can contain the universe when everything connects to everything else. The ex-pats of Quillan were willing to follow their dreams to an obscure French town, and their reward is those crystalline evenings and the murmuring mountains and a weekly market that sells the best fruit you'll ever taste. The local winery will fill any bottle you bring them from a hose. Beats sitting at home and popping another pill.

The Last Cigarette

The bus driver is smoking. There are no passengers on the bus; it's not scheduled to leave for another ten minutes. The window is open beside him, the smoke curling in the warm breeze. It's not even eight in the morning, and already the sun is pounding the cracked dirt and hot asphalt, the sky as fiercely blue as it was yesterday, as it will be tomorrow. Yesterday, a fire swept over the hills, visible from our neighbour's patio, and we watched planes buzz overhead, dropping precious water in bright curtains while the tiny figures of men in orange jackets struggled with heavy hoses.

They do that, in France. The bus driver wants to smoke; let him smoke! In Canada, in Vancouver, he'd be fired. He'd be vilified and reviled, crucified by public opinion. Smoking is the worst thing a person can do in Vancouver - if it's a cigarette, that is. The parks and sidewalks of summer are heavy with the reek of marijuana, and the steps of the police station make a handy stoop for those who prefer to smoke crack. In Vancouver, only legal drugs are frowned on.

It's different in France, where they take pleasure seriously.

It should be frivolous, but somehow it's not. It's humane. It's a recognition of the bus driver as a man, not as a functionary of some social class, or even as a representative of the company that pays him. Let them eat cake, as Marie Antoinette never said, being ten years old when Rousseau wrote the line in his Confessions. The much vaunted French rudeness - something, I hasten to add, we have never experienced

- may come down to this. For visitors from more service-oriented cultures, like that of North America, the snobbish French waiter is an archetype. But in France, no one expects servility, from anyone. When they talk of *egalite*, they mean it. Note that this is not the same as the equality an American might strive for. Obama, a Harvard-educated law professor, spoke on the campaign trail in a transparently affected manner; "folks are drillin'," and so on. Donald Trump's vocabulary is far more limited now as a President than it was when he was merely a billionaire. In America, being a man of the people is seen as desirable, at least if you want to get elected. But in France, egalite means that everyone is a king.

This is changing, as all things must. The French are more resistant than most to the flattening of the world that's going on all around us, chewing up cultures while we sleep at night. But France in 2017 is not the same as France in 2007, let alone the France of 1957. And I won't deny the utter frustration of living here, when your wife needs sanitary pads unexpectedly and every store in a good-sized city is closed because it's Sunday. What is charming to a tourist can become a nightmare for a resident. And we, with our six-month stints here and there across Europe, fall right into the gap between the two.

I know smoking's terrible. I don't do it myself. But then, I do more than my share of drinking, and that's not doctor recommended either. No one wants a bus that reeks of second-hand smoke, and I'm old enough to remember when going to the pub meant days of your clothes reeking with the lingering acid stench of other people's smoke. I know why the rules are as they are. But it will be a shame when the French stop taking two to three-hour lunch breaks on a workday. It will be a pity when someone reports the bus driver for smoking inside the bus, removing a little more pleasure from the life of a stranger. Personal liberty ends where the rights of others begin, and I know that, but it seems sometimes that we're all simultaneously expanding the bubbles we live in while demanding that everyone else's shrink to accommodate us. You will by now have noticed that this is no longer about smoking. To which I would reply it never really was.

Cultures die slowly. But they do die. The last time I was in England, I was struck by the changes in my old home town. If ever there was a place that could do with some change, Coventry was it. But there's just something so...American about the brightly colored bars, the gastro-pubs, the shopping malls hulking on the edge of town. And I have no problem with America, either. I just don't want to see it in England. Besides, we can blame America all we want, but they'd close Disneyland Paris in months if it stopped making money. We all pretend to despise what we think we should, but someone's buying those Nickelback albums. Someone's keeping up with the Kardashians. In Venice, some wit had spray-painted a carefully stenciled Magic Castle on the wall of one of the narrow streets, with the legend Disneyland Venice below it in Disney's trademark font. But I was a tourist there too. Complain about the crowds all you want, but every person in the faceless crowd has as much right to be there as you do. And American culture wouldn't have achieved its international dominance if people didn't like it. Once upon a time, Britain ruled the world, but the nations of Europe didn't adopt tea and cricket the way they have hamburgers and Starbucks.

When the French start to put business before pleasure, all we'll have is another Anglo-Saxon country. And something irreplaceable will be lost when the bus driver stubs out his last cigarette.

Anastylosis

It's not that I didn't want to go to Warsaw. It's just that I'd heard Krakow was better. But we go where the budget airlines will take us. We go where we can afford to go. And any new place has its appeal. I generally find something to like about every European city I've visited. So we went to Warsaw anyhow.

You can see the ravages of war across Europe, from the bullet holes in the walls of the church in Marseille to the bodies of dead Nazis still turning up in Russian fields. My home town was never occupied, but still bears the scars of brutal bombing raids. But few cities suffered what Warsaw did. The war in the West, for all its horror, was positively genteel compared to the Eastern Front that rolled through Poland. In 1944, with the German dream of Lebensraum disappearing under an unstoppable tide of Red Army soldiers, the Polish resistance saw their chance to free themselves from Nazi rule. For two months, the men and women of the Resistance fought in the ruins of their shattered city with a bravery that beggars belief. But all the courage in the world wasn't enough to save the city. The uprising was crushed, and the Nazi reprisal was merciless. Warsaw was obliterated. Systematically, methodically, sadistically, the Nazis demolished the city building by building. A metropolis of 1.3 million became a ghostly ruin where less than a thousand people clung to life amid the rubble and the stench of death.

So far, so horrifying. But the remarkable thing about Warsaw is its resurrection. The Old Town was painstakingly recreated, just as it was before the war, so now you can wander the cobbled streets and admire the historic architecture and forget that these things ever happened. Only an informed eye might notice that these historic buildings are just a little too well-preserved. A little too intact.

It's called anastylosis, the act of rebuilding the ruins of the past, using the original materials wherever possible. It's something I think about a lot. The old conundrum of the Ship of Theseus. The buildings of Warsaw's Old Town are mostly younger than my father is. Does that make them somehow less authentic? Is replacing one brick at a time better than doing it all at once, and if so, why? The Colosseum in Rome is two thousand years old, but most of what you see now is far younger than that. Reconstructed. Restored. Fake, in a sense.

I think about this in Warsaw. I think about it in Rome. I think about it in Niaux cave in the south of France, where the paintings on the walls are tens of thousands of years old. At Chauvet, at Lascaux, the more famous painted caves, they've built an exact replica of the cave system for tourists to visit. The original caves are closed, the prehistoric paintings in danger of being polluted by the breath of the people who come to see them.

I think of this every time a cut heals. I think of how every cell in my body replaces itself with an imperfect copy. Even our scars are merely copies of the original wound, and the person you'll be in ten years will have none of the parts you have now. We're not the real thing. We're copies of ourselves.

Warsaw is still Warsaw, despite everything it's been through. The reconstructed Old Town, with its colorful buildings and atmospheric alleys, is as charming as any in Europe. And it remains shockingly affordable. A 500ml bottle of beer cost 50 cents in the grocery store. A big meal for two, with starter and dessert and a couple of drinks, can be had for $25-30. Warsaw's not as popular as Krakow is with tourists, but it's a great place for a budget-minded traveler to visit. It may be a reconstruction, but it's as real and authentic as any other city. And it's just as beautiful, too. Maybe even more so, once you know what it took to make it that way. The city stands as a triumph of beauty against all the odds. A monument to the human capacity for regeneration. Maybe the bravery and tenacity and resilience of its people is the most beautiful thing of all.

Prague: Fear and Beauty

We came late to Prague. By the time we made our way to the red-roofed city, the path to the east had already been well beaten by hordes of budget travelers and lairy British stag parties. An influx of foreign tourists has pushed Prague close to the top of the list of Europe's most visited cities, with all the opportunities and problems that kind of popularity creates for the local residents.

But Prague is every bit as beautiful as it was back when it seemed so exotic, smiling shyly behind the Iron Curtain. The Hausmannian grandeur of the Old Town buildings invites comparison with Paris, but Parisiens would never allow their buildings to be painted like this. Bright yellow next to powder blue beside terracotta. And while tourists gape at the astronomical clock that jerks into life twenty-four times a day, the sun - when it shines - gilds the dark spires of the Church of Our Lady of Tyn and makes the old stones glow as brightly as the painted buildings.

The same force that makes a person wander the world pushes flowers from the ground to salute the distant sun. The artists of Prague don't stop painting the old buildings just because they can no longer afford to own them. Among the graffiti of the Old Town, two themes recurred: the Golem, as played by Paul Wegener in the 1920 horror film he directed. And the simple phrase, in English: Life Is Beautiful.

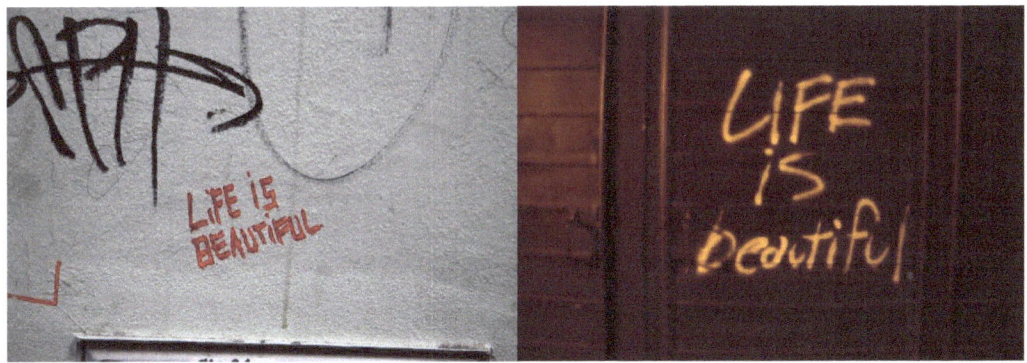

Flowers bloom and die and never leave a mark, and for most of us, this beautiful life is the same. Few of us shape history, like the dead kings in their cold tombs on the high hill where Prague's castle stands. But that doesn't keep us from trying. For an additional fee that's as steep as the stairs, you can climb the tower of St Vitus Cathedral and look out across the river at Prague. And up there, in the teeth of the wind that rises from the Vltava, you can see the old stones scored with the initials of decades of visitors, the merged letters in a dozen languages forming the ridges and valleys of an insensate fingerprint.

Prague isn't as cheap as it used to be, when the first intrepid tourists arrived from the West after the fall of Communism. But it's still an absolute steal compared to the likes of Paris or London or Barcelona. Two nights at the gorgeous five star Art Nouveau Palace cost 166 euros after tax. Dinner and drinks for two at a Michelin starred restaurant for €200. Prague still represents a great deal for a budget traveler, and offers a chance to splash out on high-end experiences at a price you could never hope to pay in other European capitals.

Prague has other marks, too. Scars with gloomier origins than the vandalizing initials of bright and brutish tourists.

On the day we visited, a young woman was lighting a candle in front of the narrow window of the church basement. The stone is still pockmarked with holes, where Nazi bullets once struck sparks from the walls. Seven hundred and fifty soldiers launched attack after attack on the church, but couldn't dislodge the men hiding inside. After hours of fighting, the Germans brought in the fire brigade and ordered them to flood the basement. Not one of the Czech freedom fighters was taken alive. The mission cost them their lives, and the lives of anyone connected to them. It also prompted Nazi massacres in villages entirely unconnected with the plot. But it was the only successful assassination of a high-ranking Nazi officer. The war would continue, of course, with or without Reinhard Heydrich, Hitler's 'man with an iron heart.' But at the cost of their lives, Josef Gabcik, Jan Kubis, Adolf Opalka, Josef Bublik, Jaroslav Svarc, Josef Valcik, and Jan Hruby proved that despite their military prowess, even the highest ranking officials of the Nazi government could be killed. And 70 years later, Czechs still honor the bravery of men willing to die for their country. Some fights are worth having. And life is beautiful. So beautiful that sometimes it's worth losing.

Prague feels like a place with secrets. It's still relatively new to modern mass tourism, having been shut off behind the Iron Curtain within my lifetime. You can see it in the bullet marks, or in the creepy statue of the Commendatore outside the theater where Mozart's Don Giovanni premiered. You can see it in the frowning face of the ubiquitous Golem. Stories make cities what they are, just as they do for people. We become the total of what we experience, our cathedrals and our bullet holes. Our spires and basements. We may be the richest and most fortunate group of people in human history, and yet so many of us are afraid. Afraid to lose what we have. Afraid to fail. Afraid of others who are themselves prisoners of fear, that makes them lash out and bite anyone they can reach. Fear lives at the heart of our culture, the magic word written down and stuffed into the hollow clay skull of the Golem to make it live.

Tyranny comes in many forms, and fear has always been one of its favorite weapons. Prisons without bars are the hardest to escape. I'm living proof that you can spend your whole life making what seems like the right decision and never get any closer to what you really want - the raw experience of being alive. Inside each of us, an iron-hearted voice commands caution, and while we hoard worthless tokens and live in fear of losing, we miss the bright imperfect world sailing by.

And yet we all want to make our mark. That brief blaze of light across an immensity of darkness, to say in some way to the uncaring universe that we were here. This is mine, a few words held out into the world like writing on water, vanishing even in the act of creation. The rough wind whirls the ticket from my hand, and I carry on without it, lighter for the loss.

Fascinada

His father built this boat. With tools worn by time and help from his uncle, he bent the planks around the frame and hammered them into place and sealed the joints with hot pitch, while the summer light bent and warped in the haze of heat that rose from the metal can. Every year afterwards, in July heat, he rowed the boat from the village to the island to heave rocks into the bay and keep the church afloat.

This year, the old man is too sick to row out to the church. Too sick even to ride in the bow over the sleek skin of the sea and watch his son pull back on the oars. This year, the son will go alone and heave rocks into a bay filled with rocks to honour a God he barely believes in.

*

On the day of the Fascinada, I was riding in a speedboat across Boka Bay. My skin, tanned and discolored already from a bright Italian winter, crackled under the assault of Montenegrin sun and salt. The bus we had taken from Dubrovnik to Kotor had been held up for hours at the border, and we had missed the tour we had booked. We found another and coughed up our money, assured by the guide that we'd make it back to the dock with plenty of time to catch the bus back to Croatia. It was a truncated visit to Montenegro already, made even shorter by the long wait at the border.

And as the rowboats began to congregate in the ancient harbour of Perast, decked out in flags in honour of the sacred occasion, we were bouncing across the bay with the thrum of the engine loud in our ears, anxiously watching the clock as the minutes ticked by. We couldn't spend a night in Kotor. The trip was already costing us more than we could afford. We had to make it to our bus, the final bus to leave that day. And the departure time crept closer and closer. This is how, incidentally, life gets lost to us. Minute by minute, while we're looking elsewhere.

*

In Capri, they charge you 12 Euros to lie flat in a musty rowboat and be hauled into the Blue Grotto. It's a tourist trap, no question of that. But it manages to be just about worth it still. Lit by the sun outside, the water in the dripping cave is an unearthly, unreal blue, as though reality has been Photoshopped by a happy quirk of geology and physics. Romans made this place a shrine, and it's easy to see why even today, as the tour boats follow each other around the walls and the owners belt out Sole Mio for tips while cameras flash and chime. The water is startlingly clear, making it seem far more shallow than it actually is, and you want to dive into it the way a bird seeks the open sky, its throat swelling with song. But you're not supposed to. The emperor Tiberius used to swim here, along with his retinue of boys. But you're no emperor, and it's not for you.

Of course, people do swim there. They come at night when the tours aren't running and climb down the steep steps carved into the cliff outside, their towels rolled in their hands. But swimming at night makes me uneasy. And the waters around Capri, made inviting by iridescent colour and clarity, are chilly in March. For our first six months in Italy, the winter months, we never swam.

"Look!"

From the deck of the bobbing boat, the skipper held out his phone to show the image of the two of us glowing on the screen. Floating in the water, our bodies were perfectly visible from head to toe, skin turned a bright, almost neon blue by the water's weird effect. "Like Smurf!" he cried, as though delighted by a phenomenon he must have seen hundreds of times before. "Like Papa Smurf!"

The blue caves of Kotor don't have the same restrictions as the one on Capri. They don't have the same tourist pressures, either. This small country, younger than my brother's daughter, can't afford to be as strict with its tourists as Italy can. The chance to leap into the Gatorade-coloured water we had seen in Italy was a big part of the reason we had wanted to take a boat trip in Montenegro. The water in the cave at Kotor, our leather-skinned skipper told us in charmingly inaccurate English, is eight meters deep. But it's so clear that you kick your legs carefully as you tread water, certain that your feet will scrape the rocky bottom. It's a disorientating feeling, floating in the middle of the bright blue nothingness, held up by the taste of salt in your throat.

*

Five hundred and sixty-five years to the day before we swam in the blue cave, two brothers - they weren't Montenegrin, because there was no Montenegro then - went fishing in the bright blue bay that sustained their village. One of the brothers had been sick a long time, his face grown gaunt and angular, his rough fingers trembling as he stared out to sea. But rowing and hauling traps up from the clear depths is work for two men, not one, and so they set out together.

In the bay they had known their whole lives, they found something new. A pile of rocks, rising out of the ocean, bearing an icon of the Madonna and child. I imagine the brothers falling to their knees as the pellucid waves lapped against the tight planks of the boat they built by hand, overcome that God should reveal himself to them. And when the sick man began to get better after this minor miracle, the brothers could hardly have been surprised. Miracles tend to follow one another.

When fishermen from Perast returned safe from the sea, they would drop a rock into the bay where the icon appeared, to give thanks. A pile became a mound, and a mound became a hill, and in the bay, an island formed. The church built on the island founded on fishermen's thanks is still there today.

The church was the last stop on our tour of the bay, and the one that interested us least. Forest fires blazed on the surrounding mountains, and the bus we had to catch might already be in the station, and we stared across the water as though we could make the harbour come closer through force of will alone. While the other members of our tour explored the small church, we stayed close to the boat, eager to leave.

Jacinta Kunic-Mijovic spent twenty-five years waiting for her husband to return from the sea that took him from her. While she waited, she sewed a tapestry for the church. She sewed for twenty-five years until she lost her sight. She threaded her own hair into the tapestry, using it to make the hair of the angels she embroidered, and if you look closely, you can see her hair turn from brown to white as the years passed, and her husband stayed lost.

It's possible that none of this actually happened. That doesn't mean it's not true.

*

I don't go in much for social media, despite being right in the middle of the curve of their demographics. But none of that makes me immune to the modern sickness. The constant wondering what's next, the inability to ever truly experience the present moment. As the waves splashed against the fiberglass hull of our boat, the mountains beginning to glow as the sun sank over the water, I was thinking about ways to boost my sales. I don't spend too much time in the past - not my own, anyway. I visit when I have to; I can't stand the smell in those places. The future is my poison. It's always tomorrow for me, or next week, or next year. Even though life has repeatedly taught me otherwise, I struggle to free myself of the feeling that if I only think hard enough, I'll come up with a plan so perfect that every moment of my life will become poetry. But of course, when the future arrives, it comes in the guise of the present, and so you're never really in it, either. The horizon moves as you approach it, and you may as well chase your own tail. Life becomes poetry the minute you live it fully, in the only time that will ever be available to you: right now.

*

We made it to our bus, in the end. We stumbled panting into the station with sweat running down our faces just as the battered old coach swung into the parking lot. The same bus, with the same weary driver and harried conductor that had carried us out of Dubrovnik at seven that morning. Relieved and dripping, we boarded, and the bus pulled out of Kotor just as the first boats rowed out of the harbour at Perast in continuation of a tradition older than Columbus' voyage. It was midnight before we made it back to the hotel bed we had left at five that morning, and by then the boats in Perast had dropped their rocks and headed home. The long-dead brother's promise to their God, kept on their behalf for half a millennium. Some people find a sense of timelessness in religion, the time-worn rites aimed at honouring or appeasing this or that personified abstraction. Some find it in motion, in breathless exertion, on the track or on the sporting field. Some find it in family. Nabokov insisted it could be found in a meadow full of butterflies.

But for me, lazy agnostic and nomadic hack, the best way I know to cut through the constant chatter of passing time and be in the eternal moment is this, hunched over a piece of paper with a pen in my grip. Everything else, be it majesty or terror, withers and shrinks the moment I reach out my hand.

Monaco: All The Money in the World

Even the toilet has a beautiful view. The window is open, and the smell of the bright sea drifts in to mingle with the faint tang of ancient piss. Down below, the Rock, the old citadel of the Grimaldi family, juts out into the Mediterranean. Red roofs glow above the white walls. The sun shines on the sheer cliff face on which the old city of Monaco sits, turning the bare rock a blinding white. I finish and zip up and step out with dripping hands, back into the sun.

A city, or a state, or a city-state, couldn't ask for a better setting. When the original Grimaldi, a crafty chancer from Genoa, came across this place, he would have been struck by the bright beauty of it, the crumpled white mountains that loom over the crystal clear sea. He would have been struck even more by its strategic position that would allow him to launch attacks against rival aristocratic families in Italy and elsewhere. His descendants still rule the tiny country, completely surrounded now by France, forced like an insect to produce dynastic heirs to avoid being swallowed up by their more powerful neighbour. The world abounds in prisons. At least this one is beautiful.

Before France was France, before Monaco was Monaco, before any idea of a nation-state existed, men and women hunted in these rocky crags and fished these jewel-bright seas. There were no borders. They carved tools from stone and buried their dead in caves and sang songs that did not survive. The animals they hunted and the world they inhabited are gone now, too. In a cliffside garden where the plants bristle with thorns, a two-room museum holds the bones of our distant ancestors, their bald skulls decorated with red ochre and seashells as they yawn silently up from under glass. A woman and a child buried together. A man taller than me. Under the sightless gaze of a reassembled mammoth, they gather dust in transparent coffins marked 'do not touch.'

Monaco is very beautiful. The stones of the old castle look as though they were laid yesterday. The cathedral gleams, freshly scoured to greet the ever-present sun. The old cobbled streets are like those of Nice, of Cannes, of Antibes. But they feel unreal. Europe by way of Disney, or worse, Las Vegas. A streetcorner Elvis hustling for tourist's change. The Lamborghinis and Ferraris that roar through the streets only add to the dreamlike unreality of the place. This isn't a country. It's a geopolitical oddity. An answer to a trivia question. A playground for the rich of every nation, its harbours bristling with ostentatious yachts all trying to outdo one another.

Of course, the old town isn't the heart of Monaco. It's a tiny warren of cafes and souvenir shops designed solely for tourists. The Grimaldis have their palace here, but how often are they home? The Monaco we have heard of, the Monaco we think we know, is down the hill, near the sea. It's at the casino.

The Monte Carlo casino sits with its back to the ocean. Small turrets sprout from the green-rusted dome of the roof. A huge round mirror on the front lawn reflects the bright blue sky, framed by swaying palm trees. The parking in front is limited, and filled with cars few can afford. Tourists pose in front of Rolls Royces and Porches, snapping selfies as though the offensively expensive cars are theirs. Born ass-kissers, impressed by nothing more than being told that they should be. This sycophantic fawning is the basis of monarchy, so it's no wonder that the tiny principality encourages this special shade of spinelessness. But I'll blow five euros on slots just to say I did.

Security guards stand at the top of the steps that lead to the casino's front door, passing groaning wands over those who try and enter. Not, perhaps, the luxury experience you were hoping for. They have the bored bovine gaze of the mouth-breathers at your local airport, passing their lobotomized stare over a faceless and shifting crowd. Residents of Monaco are prohibited by law from entering. But we pass the test. Zipping our bags closed again, we step through the door into the casino.

It's unfashionable to criticize the rich. In the absence of any higher morality, getting money becomes its own justification. So go ahead and get that money, if you can. So long as you are ready to acknowledge what that means. You can go to all the charity galas and donate to every fashionable cause you can find, and you'll be doing far more for the world than I do. But to drive a car worth half a million euros or more is obscene. The rich are welcome in Monte Carlo. It's their losses at the poker table and the roulette wheel that pay for the upkeep of these beautiful old buildings. And rich people need the excitement. The poor don't need Monte Carlo. They gamble every day of their lives. Because this is a world where the money flows up, never down, and pretty princesses expire in the wreckage of crashed cars.

The lobby is beautiful, in the way of old buildings throughout Europe. High ceilings. Noble columns. The blue sky outside turns greenish through the stained windows. Fake plants climb the pillars. Perhaps they intended a tropical feel, like the overgrown greenhouse at a botanical garden. It feels more like an aquarium where we swim slowly though the turgid emerald air. But the birdsong is a nice touch. It's only when you look up, into the cages that hang from the roof, that you see the truth. There are no birds. The hanging cages contain iPads, each overpriced screen displaying a video of a singing bird as it sways from the unreachable roof.

When the lights go out in the museum on the hill, the skeletons don't come to life. Dead for twenty thousand years now, they'll stay that way forever, frozen under glass. And the status symbols they accrued in life - seashells and flint tools and carved deer antlers - are locked up in glass cabinets, carefully labeled and artfully lit to be gawked at by schoolchildren who'd rather be anywhere else. For those who will never buy a yacht and sail the French Riviera, there's comfort in knowing that in the long run, the very long run, all the money in the world amounts to no more than a handful of decorated shells.

The Albanian Maneuver

"Too much."

"Too much?"

The gas station attendant thumbed through the crumpled bills stuffed into an envelope he held and shrugged. More lek. The last thing we needed was more Albanian currency. We were leaving the country in an hour. The car didn't need much gas, but the rental agreement demanded it be returned with a full tank. The €50 note I had given him glowed red in the midst of the pale blue Albanian money.

"Let me see if I have anything else," I said. The man shrugged again as I turned towards the door. His dark eyes gave no sign that he understood a word I was saying.

A was waiting in the car, the windows lowered in the intense heat. She handed me a €20 note, and I returned to the store and gave it to the man inside. He gave me my change in lek, useless to me except as a souvenir. Then he stared impassively at me as I waited.

"And my 50," I said.

He shrugged. He didn't understand.

Reaching across the table between us, I slid my hand into the envelope and pulled out my conspicuous €50 note. He smiled at me, as though it had slipped his mind. In a country where the average monthly income is €330, it was hard to believe. But you can't blame a man for trying. Inwardly congratulating myself on my street smarts, I headed back to the car and drove away.

*

We don't get scammed often. I've lived my whole life in cities, often in less than glamorous areas. You learn how to watch your back, watch your pockets, watch the eyes of the people around you. No, I won't sign your petition. No, I don't want a plastic flower for free. Get the fuck away from me with that friendship bracelet. But no one's immune. Once, in Paris, we were taken in by the official-looking ID of a man near the ticket machine who told us the equipment was broken and offered to sell us tickets for cash. It's easy to see the scam now, but when you're rushing for a train, bad decisions are easy to make. Still, being taken only once in all the time we've spent as tourists isn't bad. Sometimes on our travels, we'd see other people with their arms festooned with friendship bracelets, clutching plastic roses that may as well be a sign for every hustler in the city that reads, 'this person's an easy mark.' And we would smile smugly, secure in the knowledge that we were smarter than that.

But Albania beat us.

*

"Where did you get the petrol?"

I handed the receipt I had taken from the gas station to the tall young car rental agent at the port. His sea-colored eyes flickered over the paper, and the corners of his mouth twitched. Slowly, he shook his head.

"That makes sense," he said. "They filled the tank with air."

It was a full-service gas station. I never touched the pump myself. Pleased with myself for getting my €50 back, I never even checked the fuel gauge before driving away.

The rental agent rode with us to another gas station, where it took a full twenty minutes to top up the tank, forcing out the air with a few drops of gasoline at a time.

So why go to Albania? The country doesn't have a glowing reputation. Especially in Italy, where we were living at the time. When I told our landlord this story, he grimaced.

"I'm not surprised," he said.

Back in the 1990s, after the collapse of the communist government, Europe was flooded with Albanian immigrants. The country was run by a corrupt regime that allowed organized crime to flourish and prompted many Albanians to move to the West. Finally, civil war broke out in 1997, causing even more Albanians to flee. And as will happen with immigrant communities, some people turn to crime. You can still see the legacy of this lawlessness in the ubiquitous Mercedes on Albanian streets, often stolen in Germany by criminal gangs and sent back home. They joke in Germany that there's no need to bring your car on holiday with you to Albania. By the time you arrive, your car will already be there.

But Albania is beautiful. And the poverty of the country, along with its long isolation from the rest of the world, means that its Adriatic coastline is largely unspoiled. In many ways, Albania is where Croatia was a few decades ago, before foreign cruise ships began to arrive and pump money into the coastal towns.

It's not going to stay this way forever. If Albania achieves its goal of joining the EU, expect the country to experience a tourist boom as Western Europeans discover just how far their Euros go. Albania is cheap enough to make neighboring Greece seem expensive. And it has the same gorgeous weather, the same glittering sea. I don't regret visiting this up-and-coming country, even if it did cost me a little more than it should have.

So visit Albania, if you get the chance. While it still has the gleam of the undiscovered. Just keep your wits about you if you do.

Our Paris

There's nothing left to say about Paris. Not now, after a thousand years and more. Half the world's greatest writers lived here, at one point or another. Their names, etched in stone and stained with traffic fumes, loom on corners above indifferent crowds throughout the city. Books have been written. Torrents of words in a hundred languages have been splashed all over the worn cobblestones. Paris is one of those cities, like London, like Rome, where you feel the past pressing down on you. Time, in quantity, works the same way distance does, turning terror to beauty, the mundane to the profound. The mountain you stand on has nothing to do with the one you saw from the valley. We'll come back to this.

We've been to Paris before. A few years back, now. We rode to the top of the Eiffel Tower, strolled the Champs Elysee, wandered through the catacombs. It was our first time. We swore then that, if we ever came back, we'd do it differently. No tourist attractions. It was November then, and cold, and we were sick and we were tired. We couldn't shake the cold we shared, any more than we could shake the feeling that we'd missed something. Something subtle but crucial. Paris. You can miss it all, if you don't pay attention.

While my girlfriend - it sounds funny to call her that now, after the wedding - lay in bed nursing her cold, I pretended I was going to the supermarket. Instead, I found a jeweller. The woman who had the best English of all the staff smiled when I told her it was our first time in Paris. "So you will be back," she said. A statement of fact, not a question. She was right.

The thing is, if you're in Paris for the first time, you have to see the sights. Get your photos of the Arc de Triomphe, lit by golden floodlights and a thousand circling cars. Get extorted for a glass of champagne at the top of the Tower, because it will make her smile. Bathe in the gorgeous coloured light of Notre Dame. Be entirely unashamed. Be a tourist. Don't apologize for it. And once you've done all that, forget it.

Because Paris is massive, in space and in time and in the shadow it casts. It has room for you, too. And you belong here, just as much as Hemingway and Moliere, Becket and Voltaire, Joyce and Proust. There's a Paris made just for you. It will work its pernicious charm on you, just as it has on the millions that came before you, the broad streets shining wetly between the humped gray backs of cetacean buildings, the elegant streetlights reflected in glossy piles of fallen leaves.

No sights this time; we barely left the Left Bank. In the Jardin de Luxembourg, I read an essay by Joseph Roth, a few minutes walk from the vanished hotel he spent his last years in. That was the best part of a century ago. But the children still rent artfully painted wooden sailboats in the park and push them with long poles out onto the pond's green surface, just the way the long-dead writer describes. Puppets still prance and chatter on a curtained stage. Roth's world is gone, like so many others, a hundred different Parises slipping away in an infinite curve like the weird space between two mirrors. But the past lives on. The grandchildren of the children Roth described rent their toy boats from the grandson of the man who used to make them. That's my Paris. Drinking pastis in Cafe Tournon, prowling the shelves at Shakespeare and Company, eating a leisurely lunch on the Boulevard Saint Michel. It doesn't have to be yours.

Paris is no mirror. But when it rains - and it often rains, even in August - the streets shine. One of the more profound lessons travel will teach you is that we bring our own world with us. I've never come across the famous Parisian rudeness. This is a living city, the proud capital of a powerful nation, and the French feel no need to bow and scrape for tourist dollars. But I've always found respect to be a two-way street. Say "Bonjour" to everyone you interact with. That small thing alone will put you ahead of half of Paris' thirty million annual visitors.

I read once of a cow that walked all the way through Rumi's Baghdad and saw nothing, other than a bale of hay that fell from a wagon. We see what we look for, in Paris and elsewhere. It's that simple, and that complex. And in a city as old and as storied as this one, you'd hardly be surprised to find, at the turn of the next winding street, a fin de siecle boulevardier, or a veteran of Napoleon's Russian campaign, or a medieval monk clutching a rosary against his cassock. The veil between those worlds and ours is almost transparent. That, for me, is part of what gives Paris its melancholy glow. But for you, it'll be different. Your mountains and your valleys are different from mine. It was my Paris, for a week in 2014 and a couple of days in 2017. When you go, next time you go, it will be all yours.

Palermo, That's All

I don't tell those kinds of stories. You know the ones. The Three Drunk Norwegians. The Narcotrafficantes Who Chased Me Through The Jungle That Time. The Multigenerational Balinese Family Who Taught Me How To Love. Is there any greater bore than a travel bore? I can see myself even now, desperately checking my phone for messages while some pompous narcissist drones on about how in Mongolia, like, everything was like, four-dimensional. They talk about travel broadening the mind, but I see people's focus narrowing constantly, shrinking with every border they cross until every country merges into the others and all that remains in the bright bare circle of focus is themselves.

So no adventures. No mishaps. I know. You like the narrative. The metronomic propulsion that pulls your hazy attention through the forest of words between blaring notifications from your electronic narcotic of choice. Our brains are attuned to story, wired to spark at the first hint of plot, of intrigue. That's not life, though. We try, consciously or not, to experience it that way. But it isn't the truth. Sometimes things happen. Sometimes nothing happens. One means no more than the other, and both mean nothing. B doesn't follow A without our hands to guide it.

Palermo is bursting. With beauty, with colour, with charm, with life. In the crowded markets, you keep your hands in your pockets while traders sing in dialect and Sicilians push past each other. The Vucciria, Palermo's most famous market, isn't what it was when Guttoso painted it. Now it's mostly Chinese-made tat to swindle tourists. But the name has become a synonym for chaos in Sicily - "this is an absolute Vucciria!"- and a visit to a less well-known market will quickly show you why.

The traders aren't friendly. They aren't delighted to share the produce of the region with you. Here, they don't let you pick your own fruit. Tell them what you want, and they decide what you get. The gorgeous fruit at the front of the stall is only for display. It's not for you. I get it. This isn't a tourist attraction. These people are trying to earn.

Sicily doesn't have the greatest reputation. In Italy's deprived South, the Mezzogiorno, Sicily may be the most deprived place of all. And even though Garibaldi's unification of Italy started here, right in Palermo, many Sicilians don't think of themselves as Italian at all.

I'm not going to pretend that I don't immediately think of the mafia when Sicily is mentioned. And maybe it's true that as little as twenty years ago, no one even dared speak the word. But that's not true any more. Bobble-headed figures of Don Corleone sit on the shelves of tacky souvenir shops right next to similar figures of the Pope. This far from Rome, Francis I may as well be a fictional character. But the Godfather is very real. You can see it in the development boom that has made the outskirts of the city look like a pile of dominoes. Identikit empty buildings stacked up row upon row with no one inside them. You can see it in the hush of the streets away from the tourist areas, where the buildings sag against one another, reeling ruins ready to collapse. You feel it when you spend an hour in a restaurant at dinner time on a weekend and no other customers come by, as though this isn't a restaurant at all. You see it in the white-haired man standing all day in the door of an empty cafe in a crisp suit, his overcoat hanging empty-sleeved from his shoulders while he scowls out at the street.

To a Canadian, a Sicilian winter feels like summer. And I prefer cold weather to crowds. The only English we heard as we walked the streets of Palermo was three young Americans discussing "the most awesome fuckin' pizza, dude" as we passed. We visited a palazzo and paid for a tour to find ourselves the only people on it. The guide - a charming young man from the North with a mop of unruly black curls and a scattering of facial piercings - told us that Italy is rotten. Corrupt. Jobs are for those with connections, friends of friends. I advised him to marry a Canadian. Italy is shedding its young like a deer shedding its antlers, the South faster than the North. It's exactly these imbalances that brought us here, putting a comfortable Canadian existence on hold to enjoy what a still-rich but struggling economy can offer. Quality of life for a small capital outlay. Paradise at a low, low price.

And something else.

Step into the courtyard that faces the door of Palermo Cathedral, and you enter a different world. The building looks like a monument of an alien civilization, and in a way, that's exactly what it is. The Phoenicians started the building, and they're so far gone in time it's almost like they never existed. The site was developed by Greeks and Romans, Arabs and Normans, changing hands along with the island itself as successive waves of invaders conquered and fled Sicily through the centuries. The result is, for someone who has racked up more miles than most, one of the most beautiful buildings imaginable.

We ate our fruit from the market there, on a stone bench facing the church. The scarred and gnarly Sicilian oranges were the best I've ever tasted.

On our last night in Palermo, we did everything right. On the hotel's rooftop terrace, we drank sweet wine and watched the sun dip behind the mountains that crowd the city, about to push Palermo into the sea. We wandered to the Teatro Massimo and joined the surging crowd of Sicilians out for their evening stroll. We tucked into tennis-ball-sized arancini and cannoli as long as my hand. And the fractured, crumbling, corrupt city worked its charm on us. Because we like our beauty scarred. We like our cities to limp. We prefer Naples to Florence and Havana to Barcelona. It's the grit that makes the beauty shine.

And nothing happened. Palermo went on being Palermo. We went on being us.

Bastille Day In Toulouse

Carcassonne is not one city, but two. There's the modern town, with its train station and airport and supermarkets. And across the river, there's the old town. Europe's largest fortified medieval city, raising its battlements to the sky on a hill above the valley.

Never heard of it? Neither had we, until we lived close by in Quillan. But outside of Paris, Carcassonne is one of France's most popular tourist attractions. And the narrow stone-flagged streets and crcncllatcd walls makc for a charming placc to explore, even if many of the stores are given over to the usual tourist garbage.

Carcassonne is especially popular on Bastille Day, France's national holiday. Crowds cluster along the banks of the river to watch fireworks lighting up the ancient walls as though the city is under siege. But we didn't even think about Bastille Day until it was too late. By the time we started planning, there wasn't a hotel room left in the town.

Instead, we went to Toulouse.

Like so many French cities, Toulouse is a Roman town. Invaders came from the South and stamped their mark on this bend of the river, carving straight streets into the soil and raising temples to the sky. The temples are gone, but there's still something of that ancient orderliness to the town. Wherever they went, from London to Istanbul, the Romans built towns with good bones. And Toulouse's bones are exquisite, especially in the fading light of the summer sun that brings out the subtle pink of the terracotta bricks. Especially on a holiday, when the people of the city are in a mood to celebrate. Especially on Bastille Day.

Men build in stone, and as long as the stones stand, we feel the lives of those that are gone all around us. But our lives are written on water, as fragile and inconsequential as seafoam. The people pass, and newcomers take their place, and the city shifts and transforms. But the city remains.

Toulouse is a southern city. And by afternoon, the sun had pushed its way through the early clouds to make the broad river glitter. The old stones groaned as they expanded, and the city smiled. The bells chimed from the famous basilica's skeletal tower. Toulouse can be infinitely beguiling.

I'm not usually a fan of crowds. But as we made our way to the Prairie des Filtres, the grassy park on the banks of the Garonne, we could feel the excitement building. The crowd grew. Throngs of people lined both sides of the river, waiting for the show to begin. We made our way through a security checkpoint, holding open bags for hired guards to peer absently into. It's an unfortunate fact in France these days that even pleasure has to be fenced off.

French patriotism isn't like the American variety. But then, very little is. Music blared from the stage, but it was made for dancing, not marching. Tricolores were in short supply. A holiday feeling lingered under the shade trees of the park, but there was nothing specifically jingoistic about it. Maybe that's for the best. Toulouse has been the capital of a kingdom and of a distinct cultural region before France absorbed it. It's seen legions come and go, and the rosy stones they left behind no longer remember who set them on top of one another. Nations pass. But people remain.

Our first site was poorly chosen. It was right by the river, with a view of the fireworks barge. But the shade provided by the bushes, through which the fading sun fell so beautifully, made it a de facto toilet for those unwilling to cross the park and use the facilities provided. "Pardon," over and over again, as festivalgoers stepped over our legs and disappeared into the greenery. Better to pack up and find a new spot, hopefully close to the beer tent where the server complemented A's French when she ordered us drinks. Bolstered by watered-down booze, we found a new spot further back from the water and settled in to wait for nightfall.

There were no cries of "Vive la France!" as I had been half-hoping. Like most Europeans, the French keep their love of their country close to their chest. It was a fun evening, but you could be forgiven for thinking it was any other holiday. On a perfect July night, do you really need a national excuse for a party?

Unwilling to piss in a bush, we chose instead to use the bathrooms when we needed them. And it was then, in the line outside the temporary toilet block, that out of nowhere, someone began to sing the Marseillaise, and then everyone did. While massive speakers pumped out powerful bass from the stage, the crowd sang a different song entirely.

As far as overt displays of patriotism go, it was brief. But its magic was in its spontaneity, unsullied by forced participation. The people of Toulouse sang their nation's anthem because they wanted to, not because anyone was trying to make them or because they felt that they had to.

The fireworks, when they came, were impressive enough. But after that, they hardly mattered.

Piazza del Popolo

It's easy when it's like this. A perfect day under a perfect sun in my favourite place in the world. Even the puffy clouds are only there to provide a welcome break from the heat, and tourists gasp with pleasure at their tables as the light dims. They applaud when the sun comes out, as though it can hear them.

It can.

What gives the place its gorgeous melancholy glow- the edges of the cobblestones worn smooth by ten million footfalls, the marble benches rounded and softened by six hundred winters- is the lives that have been spent and vanished, never to return. The radiance of a life is visible only when it's lived as though it matters. And there I go again, putting up glass walls between the world and me.

We learn and then we forget. The rapture of that single moment, the sun setting over the dome of St Peter's or the bright day dawning over Rome's seven hills, or me here in Piazza del Popolo, glutted with sun and memory - all of this is as doomed as a spider web anchored to the wheel of a parked car. Rome can make you believe in permanence and change at one and the same time, but even the Colosseum will fall someday, long after we're already gone. And they'll build something new in its place.

I know all this, but that doesn't mean I believe it. Maybe I'm worried that I'll lose that last bit of miraculous magic I've somehow kept until now, the tiny scrap of wonder that is all that remains of my youth. It doesn't matter, but it matters to me. Maybe I'm scared that if I try to live in that wonder, that bliss, the well will one day run dry, leaving me completely and finally alone.

We don't know until we're told. The piazza would be less charming if it weren't for the Baroque masterpieces hanging in the church. The legend has it that this northern entrance to the city of Rome was haunted by demons, drawn by the presence of Nero's bones. The church they built to sanctify the square is now best known for the work of a genius with more than a touch of the devil in him. Each layer of meaning is founded on the last, Renaissance basilicas built on top of bloodsoaked pagan altars. We build the city piece by piece, just as we build the past.

I love her. That's the truth. I miss her the minute she's gone, and as all lovers must, I live in the fear that she might be taken away from me while she's somewhere I can't protect her. But love is an unknown, a big black dog I can't bring myself to trust, and even to name it seems like an incantation that will only bring misfortune and disturb dark gods. You're floating now, where the air turns to poison and the ice blooms, and no part of me can reach you. There's that fear again.

The old couple on the bench beside me are discussing Leonardo da Vinci. And one day I will be dead or widowed or divorced. But you don't start a thing by looking at its end. A symphony is not beautiful in spite of its end, but because of it. I don't write to flatter or to please. I'm not about to start now. This is not a love song. Not even now. But the wife of the couple beside me has seen me writing in English, and as she gets up to leave, she apologizes for disturbing me, and in spite of myself, I start to talk.

They were married in 1964. They honeymooned in Rome. Then and now, they climbed the many stairs to the terrace that overlooks the massive square. When they get home, the photos from now and then will sit side by side, a testament to the way the places humans build wear them out. Rome's stone bones will still stand when all three of us are dust, and the photos have all been thrown away. Rome makes you think that way. My favourite city, and hers too. For those of us who feel the breath of the dead on the back of our necks, the fading light of the past lending a golden glow to the present, there is nowhere else like it on earth.

The obelisk in the centre of Piazza Del Popolo is older even than Rome. The same spell that makes us wander through Roman homes and temples with cameras blazing made the Romans haul this monument over the sea from Egypt. Yesterday's graffiti is an eyesore that the city workers will scrub away, but the words scrawled on the walls of Pompeii are protected behind plexiglass. Time works like distance to make dirty things sacred. Climb that gorgeous mountain, and you'll find nothing at the summit but some scorched rock.

History could roll on untroubled by us, but it doesn't. The fate of the world pivots on a well-timed whisper or the sway of a skirt. It's happening right now. It will happen again.

Swimming on the Azure Coast

I'm swimming, in October.

This isn't the warm bath of the Caribbean, soaking up endless sun in between annual explosions of stormy wrath. Nor is it the ink-black, heart-stopping icewater of Vancouver. Beyond the narrow band of smooth rocks that guard the entrance to the sea, hiding just below the surf, your breath will catch as you plunge into the blue. But you will adjust. When the stolen heat of the Mediterranean sun is washed away and your core temperature more closely reflects the water's, you'll be quite comfortable.

The water is shallow for a while, the drop into the deep gradual. And if you stand up, tiny silver fish dart into the cloud of sand your feet kick up, filtering dirt and water through their mouths while you lumber past in slow motion. I've always loved the sea and cursed the fates that had me born in the English town furthest from any coast. But it's an attraction laced with fear. There are things out there against which a lone human has no defense, and even the water itself can kill. In Hawaii, they say you should never turn your back on the sea. Beautiful and deadly, a femme fatale with tight dress and drawn gun.

This isn't Hawaii either. There's no crackling coral; with ears below the water, all I hear is shifting sand. And music. I'm still hearing the melodies from last night's concert, Offenbach's Orpheus bouncing back from the white walls of the Roman amphitheater shattered by time, and the blue wavelets lift their skirts and flash bright limbs under the Riviera sun. We're lucky to be here, and don't think for a second that I don't know it. People our age are raising children, reaching for the first few rungs of the property ladder, testing at the tensile strength of their first marriages. But instead of doing that, we're pissing around on the Med.

In Canada, everything is awesome. You got a day off from work? Awesome. Your barista got your name right? Awesome. You want aioli dip with your yam fries? Awesome! When I first moved to Vancouver, it struck me as risible. Then it was comical. Then I stopped hearing it, shortly before I began to say it myself. But the thing is, some things actually are awesome, and the sea must surely be one of those things. I love it and I fear it, and far from being at odds, the two feelings feed each other. There's more to awe than love and fear, just as you need more than vermouth and gin to make a martini. But that's where it starts.

The locals here have tans that go down to the bone. That's how you can tell them from the tourists. And even in October, an hour or two on the beach will expose you to Italian, German, English, Norwegian. Without the crowds of summer, Juan les Pins still gets plenty of visitors. You only have to look at the herds of luxury yachts clustered in every harbour from here to Monte Carlo to see how blessed this peninsula is.

If you survive the threat of sharks - there are Great Whites in the Mediterranean, no matter what the tourist office says - and the much more likely sting of the beautiful and beautifully named meduse jellyfish, you'll find that the water in the showers dotted along the beach is warm from the autumn sun, at least for a little while. You could be a different person here, you start to think. You could swim every day until muscles began to show through skin tanned the colour of brandy. Your hair would bleach to the warm yellow of the sand, and your eyes would take on the bright clarity of the ocean, right there, when it rises and glitters green before bubbling over the pebbles. You'd speak mellifluous French and playfully race pretty women from one buoy to another, letting them win so that you have to buy them dinner. In the evenings, you would read Sartre and Camus and pronounce everything absurd, and you'd always be up in the morning to buy a fresh baguette from the boulangerie.

It's an idle and pleasant fantasy, something to savour while the beads of water roll off your salty skin. And you lie back on a towel, and feel the hot sand vibrate as a train rattles towards Nice, and while you rinse the seawater from your mouth with cheap red wine and dream about being a person you are not, the awesome mystery rolls along the same steel tracks, and disappears.

Heaven's Shadow

I should be good at leaving places behind. I do it often enough. Some places look their best in the rearview mirror, receding as rapidly from memory as from view.

But I like it here, in Juan les Pins. Even in the winter, with the sea cold and murky and the shutters pulled down in front of the stores. Maybe especially in the winter. There's a melancholy glow that haunts a seaside town when the tourists are all gone. My mother taught for a while at the school I attended, and when classes were over, I'd stay behind, after the other kids had gone home, and wait for her to finish work. The empty corridors felt the same way the boardwalk does in winter.

And it's just so beautiful. As beautiful as any place I've lived in a life stalked by beauty. The distant mountains seeming to bloom larger under a sky turning steadily pink. The sun sending up one last dying flame to shine in the windows of a silent minaret. The constant murmur of the sea at my side, running short of breath as it stumbles on the sand. It's that sky, the same light that bewitched Picasso and Monet, blue as mother's eyes in the afternoon, fragile pale rose when the sun begins to sink, that I'm trying to steal with a clumsy pen.

Along the promenade, shadows gather and stretch. A train rattles past, humming towards Nice. The tracks pass close to our house, following the inward curve of the bay. At night I watch the lit windows sail through the dark, a tiny wandering world in an immensity of night. But in what remains of the day, the sea is the same bright and careless blue it was when we first arrived six months ago, before the stain of winter darkened the water and sent the bathers home. Underwater in October, the rumble of passing trains could have been the groaning of restless continents as I swam, and quick silver fish gobbled at the sand my flailing feet kicked up. We can only afford to live in coastal places in the winter when it's cheaper, and after October, it got too cold to swim. But maybe it's better, once the kids have all gone home.

A ladder rattles. Joggers thump past on leaden legs, unwilling to break stride just to gawk. But some of us have time to stand and stare. I'm not the only person who

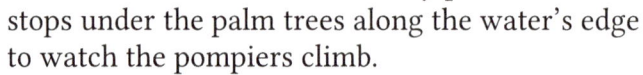

stops under the palm trees along the water's edge to watch the pompiers climb.

Dressed in dark utilitarian overalls, the firefighters in France wear huge, flawlessly shining steel helmets. Like the war gear of a dead era, sabers clutched in outstretched arms as riders charge into roaring volleys of cannon and shot. It was here, almost right here, that Napoleon landed on his return from exile, almost exactly 203 years ago.

A harsh clatter turns more heads. The pompiers have reached a second-floor balcony and are trying to prize up the metal shutter. They heave in tandem as though working the oars of a galley, here on the coast where Phoenician triremes once landed. But the shutter stubbornly resists. So one man holds the insolent metal at knee height, and the other shatters the glass pane of the door behind it. There's a merry tinkling sound as it breaks, the clinking of glasses in some lively bistro. One man ducks inside, and the other follows, and the bright helmets sink into the gloom inside the apartment. Juan les Pins looks like paradise. It feels like it too, sometimes. But tragedy, misfortune, disaster are at home here like anywhere else. Two days ago in Carcassonne, close to where we used to live before we came here, a man opened fire on police in an idyllic French village and took hostages. The sea swallows the blood that runs towards it every day. There'll be more blood tomorrow.

The light fades. The streetlights spark. Along the promenade, a child stumbles with shining eyes toward a friendly dog before his mother pulls him sharply away. Children and animals share a world that is closed to us adults. The eternal moment, the burning present that is the only thing we will ever have, and we don't see it. Is it the atrocities, the capital H horrors that some flawless fictional judge - because only fiction can be flawless - would cite to condemn us? Or is it this neglect, the casual and ubiquitous failure to pay attention to the million miracles occurring around us, at all times in all places? I'm worse than most. For me, it's always last week or next year. Blessed beyond the dreams of most people, and too self-involved to see it. Drive and ambition and focus, combined with luck, can carry you to paradise in the end, but once you get there, they'll ruin it for you. That's how it works. Our gods are demons, and our flaws are often our finest traits. The intellect that builds paradise can never enjoy it.

What makes this place so beautiful to me, so richly resonant with my own prickly personality? Not mountains and warm sky and bright blue sea. Not those alone, anyway. The crowning jewel of Juan les Pins' haunting radiance is the twin steel rails that will soon carry us away forever.

A Death in Nocera

It can't have been more than a week after we moved. We were still new to Nocera, still finding our way around. It might have been our first grocery shop, after we returned the rental car that brought us there from France.

The bells of the church were ringing wildly, the way they might have done when Saracen sailors swarmed along the valley from the nearby coast. A battered old pickup truck rolled slowly down the road, carrying a wooden A-frame covered in flowers in its bed. At the statue of Padre Pio that stands in a tiny square in front of the tabacchi, sleek horses stamped. A black carriage waited for the crowd that filed slowly down from the church. It was the second time we had moved to Italy, but it was our first funeral.

The dead are everywhere. Colour photographs of the recently deceased stare out from posters on every wall in town, announcing funerals. An Italian funeral is a very public event, one last chance for the dead to cut *la bella figura* in front of their neighbours. All are invited. Half the town might show up, walking at a snail's pace behind the coffin as it's carried to the cemetery. The graveyards look like towns in miniature, rows of mausoleums like scaled-down churches lining the railway tracks between Nocera and Pagani, between Nocera and Cava dei Terreni, between Nocera and here. For a culture so good at celebrating life, Italians make a big deal out of death.

We move every six months. Is there any better way to live? Hair bleached by constant sun, eyes burned by beauty, bellies full and hearts forever expanding. Like St. Francis's sparrows, we make our home any place warm, living off nothing but luck and an Internet connection. The steel rails expand in constant sun as they carry us from place to place, our hearts humming to the clicking of the train wheels and our minds alive with novelty.

It all sounds very glamorous. But that's not the truth. Our existence is filled with plenty of pleasures, but it's precarious. No friends. No family. No safety net, because a net is a trap where beautiful things die. Every rent payment is a challenge to be met. Every apartment is a short-term shelter, not worth the trouble to make into a home before we move on again, never to return. This is the life we have chosen, for now, and I have no complaints, for all the challenges that come with not knowing what country you'll spend Christmas in. But it's not for everyone. And this transient and uncertain life- the bad parts of it, anyway - are becoming a reality for more and more people who never chose it for themselves.

We had been living like this for a little over a year when I started to lose the beauty. The money ran low and the bills piled up, and the insecurity of it all started to weigh on me. Along the waterfront in Juan les Pins, I'd walk into the winter wind that whipped the sea into black waves and scowl at the scenery. Even Paradise has its problems. And in the heart of heaven, my dreams were haunted by the sleepless fear that now I was so close to the life I always wanted, it would all be taken away.

But the truth doesn't change with the scenery. Ego is opaque, a painted-over window that shuts out all light and shows you only your own reflection. I've always been fixated on the future, and that drive and focus got me to where I was, living a life most can only dream of. But that same focus was taking it all from me, one minute at a time.

I should have seen it in Paris, where the division between past and present is thinner than the skin on your ankles where the bugs know to bite. I should have understood, when I walked through the hushed halls of Vienna's gleaming museums, enthralled and alone. I glimpsed it in my favourite city, Rome, but never understood what I was seeing, even as I waxed lyrical about the melancholy glow of repurposed marble monuments and paving stones worn smooth by time. I couldn't see past my self. And even when I understood that I had come to prefer a life through glass, watching the world go by in a sun-scoured piazza while I interacted with nothing but the weather, I still managed to miss the truth as it sailed by on every side.

Wherever I went I found myself. We all like to laugh at those tourists who go to Italy and eat at McDonald's, missing the point completely. But we are all missing the point. The only world you can live in is the one you carry around in your head, the toxic fume of rotting memory and futile hopes and naïve dreams. And it's all this, all your aims and goals and worries and hopes and fears, that are poisoning every moment of your life.

We take photos. We share stories. We write, some of us, tales about all we've seen and done, as though you can claw back the water in a river as it flows past. Life is that river, and we are life. When we live at all, we live and die in this flow. Forever dying and forever being born. The processes that gave rise to your unique consciousness began a million years ago a million miles away, and they don't end here. In the absence of any real way to define yourself apart from the rest of the cosmos, you will find yourself forced to confront the central truth that there is no such thing as you. The bundle of memories that you lug around with you is amorphous and changeable, full of tricky lighting and weird camera angles. The past can't tell you who you are, not when you're making it up as you go along, and biologically, your memories happened to someone else anyway. Meanwhile, the future doesn't exist at all.

All that leaves is the present. And that's all you are. Your present sensations, whether pleasurable or painful, are all you will ever be. As much a part of the universe as the clouds in the sky or the notes of a song. It took me an embarrassingly long time to see the naked truth that was all around me. I had to move halfway across the world and begin an entirely new life before I could see what children know. And even after all that, I'm prone to forget.

In Nocera, the crowd followed the funeral procession through the narrow streets. At times like this, our roles seem sometimes to overwhelm us. The bereft widow, flanked by adult children, leading a procession of neighbours and well-wishers who don't know what to say. The holes in our lives that the dead leave behind, until the world leaves us behind too and the absences are forgotten by those who never knew anything else.

In Nocera, the crowd passed on, leaving the street behind it strewn with fallen flowers, all the way to the grave. No one picked them up. That, too, would be missing the point.

The best we can hope for, the best that the very best of us can do, is to leave the street behind us full of flowers.

Malta

I didn't write a word in Valletta. Not as we watched the sun sink like a sentence handed down, perched on top of the thick stone walls that have cradled the tiny city since the 1500s. Not when we wandered among the temples, some of the oldest buildings on earth, perched on cliffs above the dazzling sea. Not even when the fading light made the glass of the colourful closed balconies on every building, the gallariji, shine like smiling eyes.

It was winter in Malta, but winter in Europe's sunniest city is a fine thing. In a city like Valletta, built on a single hill threaded through with steep stone stairs, a visit in the summer heat could easily become a trial. The swimming is great in Malta, I'm told, but we weren't swimming in February.

Instead, we went to see the temples. Hagar Qim was founded over 5000 years ago, when the pyramids weren't even thought of, and mammoths hadn't yet gone extinct. Under glass in Valletta's Archaeological Museum, the carved statues and artifacts of these enigmatic sites yield few answers. They are so old that the years no longer touch them.

Malta's a unique place. And it's not just the prehistoric ruins that make it that way. The succession of foreign occupiers of the tiny nation is a poem on the rise and fall of empires. From Carthage to Rome, to Arabs to Normans, to the Spanish, the French, and the British. On the wall near our hotel, where we got upgraded to a suite for no particular reason, a painted sign proclaimed the location of a vanished victory kitchen, a community kitchen designed to help rationed food stretch further during World War II. The Maltese still speak English, but not among themselves. The Maltese language is as unique as everything else about the tiny island nation. It's the only Semitic language in Europe, descended from extinct Sicilian Arabic. And these days, plenty of Maltese residents speak Italian just as readily. It could be the weather or the scenery or the religion, but Malta feels Italian. Like some alternate universe where Italy was ruled by the British. That might be reason enough to visit by itself.

But I didn't write a word.

"Are you going to see the Michelangelos?" the dark-eyed hotel receptionist asked us as we checked in. She was talking about the other Michelangelo, Merisi, better known to history as Caravaggio. The painter fled Malta with a bounty on his head, but two of his works still hang in the ornate Co-Cathedral where we duly paid to get in. After the garish gold and Mannerist fluff of the rest of the cathedral, Caravaggio's gloomy and sparse Beheading Of St. John the Baptist is all the more striking. The massive painting is mostly black, its subjects frozen in the midst of a murder, with blood still gushing from the fallen Saint's neck and two onlookers watching through a barred window. The audience drawn into the masterpiece, no longer removed but now complicit, a 400-year-old crack in the glass between that world and this.

And still, I didn't write a word.

Not in the church. Not in the cobbled streets and narrow alleyways, nor at a café table where waiters bustled past with coffees and beers and pastizzi, the delicious pastries filled with spiced peas that I've been missing ever since we left the island.

Malta is not like anywhere else. And perhaps it's a shame that a large portion of its visitors come purely for the warm weather and warm water, and ignore the strange and rich culture of this ancient island. Or maybe not. We all enjoy what we enjoy, and there's nothing that makes an appreciation of art

history inherently superior to a nice swim. Malta's history, its language, its amazing 30 cent pastries, its city-built shelters for the army of feral cats that patrol the stony streets - it's all unique, and it's all beautiful. And I was too busy taking it all in to record any of it.

And now that a full year has come and gone between Malta and me, now that a sea far wider than the Mediterranean has been crossed and the sun no longer shines, what I keep closest from Malta is not all the things I enjoyed there and didn't write about. It's this:

Even in Malta, it rains sometimes. Caught out by a sudden shower that made a slick mirror of the pavement, we dashed through the open iron gate of a tiny courtyard between tall buildings. And stood transfixed, heedless of the cool raindrops spilling down on our heads. A single tree in the courtyard was full of sparrows. And every single bird was singing as though its tiny heart might burst with joy.

The Warsaw Dichotomy

Is the pianist good? I wouldn't know. Every driver seems skilled to someone who's never been behind the wheel. I love music, but there's not one atom of musical talent in my body. I can only look with awe at those who know how to make an instrument sing.

It's a tourist trap, I know that much. The concerts we go to, in Venice and Vienna and now in Warsaw (Ws are pronounced as Vs in Polish, so the alliteration stands) are aimed at people like us, who wouldn't know a good musician from a bad one. Like those restaurants that have menus in seven different languages, it's a bad sign.

But the music's still beautiful. Any competent player could make these works shine, and in the small room, the grand piano makes the air hum. You can feel the bass notes in the soles of your feet. Some of the tiny audience try to record the musician on their phones. But that's missing the point. Recorded, these notes are just sounds, one after another. A phone camera won't capture the candlelight. Or the audience's reverential hush. Or the moon outside, showing its pinched face through the tattered clouds. Chopin won't be the same on your laptop's crappy speakers, via some YouTube playlist. The experience is part of the magic.

We arrived at the concert straight from the Warsaw Uprising museum. Two hours of horrific history, telling the story of brave, doomed men and women battling the Nazi war machine in the shattered remnants of their homes. Stepping from that to this, shivering slightly as you shed your jacket in the warm lobby. The cobbled streets shining with rain, and the warm air and soft light, and music.

The museum has a basement. There's a tiny room, half-hidden in the gloom by a black rubber curtain that hangs in whispering strips. Inside, there's a TV screen. On that TV, there's an old man speaking horrors.

His apartment looks like every old person's apartment. The heavy wood furniture, the bright brass pendulum of a ticking clock in the background. And the man looks like any old man, with his wool sweater and black-framed glasses provided by socialized healthcare. But this man is not your grandfather. He was a German soldier who served in Warsaw during the Nazi occupation. He saw first-hand the actions of the infamous

Dirlewanger brigade, the SS penal company made up of murderers and rapists and monsters that represented the worst elements of German society. The stories he tells are appalling. At one point in the eternally looping video, the man wonders aloud, "I don't know if I should be telling you this." He should, and he does. But it's hard to hear.

And then an hour later, soft light and piano music and the applause of a civilized audience of tourists from across Europe. Sitting close to the stage, I can watch the piano's mechanism move as though breathing under the pianist's precise fingers. I can watch this machine sing, drawing out all our deepest, noblest, most tender emotions note by note.

Men make machines that can heal and kill. We all know this. The observation has been made many times. Our species throws out a Stalin with one hand and a Mandela with the other, for us to condemn and laud and align ourselves with one against the other. It's easy, when nothing's at stake. But in every heart that swells to the piano's rippling magic there lurks a vile Dirlewanger, waiting for a war to come.

It gets worse.

The last concert we attended was in Venice, in the Palazzo delle Prigioni, the Palace of Prisons. Vivaldi's Four Seasons and some Mozart. Popular classics for non-connoisseurs. It was all string music that made no use of the piano that lay covered in a corner of the stone-walled room. But that piano was donated to Venice by Hitler himself, as a sign of friendship between two Fascist states. The Nazis were barbarous, but they weren't barbarians. They admired the art they merrily looted from the people they subjugated, and adoration of Wagner was almost a religion for Hitler's court. As the Austrian Jewish writer Joseph Roth put it, "the Germans have always had the gift of killing to music." It was cultured, civilized, educated people who obliterated Warsaw and brought all Europe to ruin. And the same soul that could appreciate all that was noble and elevating in the music of Wagner could order the destruction of entire nations over lunch. The most horrifying thing about monsters is that they aren't really monsters at all. They're people, like me. Like you.

But music can be like a guided meditation sometimes, turning one's thoughts in directions they wouldn't normally go. This tunnel looks the same from either end. Murderers love music. Music moves murderers. Warsaw, reduced to rubble by retreating German forces in an act of staggering vindictiveness, has been rebuilt. The Old Town, the Stare Miasto, is as charming as any in Europe. They're still playing Chopin, night after night, right where the barricades stood in 1944. And if the worn cobbles of the streets still remember the blood that once washed over them, they must also remember the nights like this, with a candle in the window and music in the moon-bright air. Pain can last a lifetime, or more, echoing like a curse down through the generations. But beauty is forever.

For J

The nights in Campania were almost always perfect. If the storm clouds stayed away, the sun lingered behind the volcano, turning the mountain purple while the sky above it darkened. In time our shadows disappeared. Stars smiled. A poison candle guttered on the table, its fumes turning away mosquitoes. Fireworks crackled above the town, almost every night. The amber flame flickered in a thousand tiny versions formed by the beads of condensation on the skin of my wine glass.

And we talked late into the night, while a yellow comet crackled overhead and the sun shifted below our feet. I remember the night you were born, and nothing makes me feel older than the fact that you are now a young woman, with a mind sharper than mine ever was and a heart more open than mine will ever be again. I used to be sixteen. But that was before you were born. Years have a way of filing off the more tender parts of ourselves, a thread recoiling from the candle before ever touching the flame. When I was your age, the world used to talk to me, the way it does to you. But somewhere along the way, I lost the ability to hear it. This isn't a tragedy; I got it back. It just took a lot of years and a lot of miles. Under the glowering volcano, I relearned what I knew when I was your age.

But you get it. And by it, I mean everything. When I was your age, I was miserable. It seemed impossible to reconcile the beauty I glimpsed like a sky through bars with the life the world seemed designed to force me into. Feathers sticky with blood clinging to the cleaver; the abattoir floor littered with severed wings. I was hopeless. I listened to other people too much, and they told me that the best years of my life were already behind me. Of course they were wrong. The bright sun and deep nights of Campania prove that. For that matter, so did Vancouver. When I was your age, I never imagined that life would be as beautiful and as strange as it has been. Even with the losses we all inevitably accrue as the years skulk past. Because of those losses, not in spite of them.

I hope you know that.

We had fun during your visit; at least, I think so. I did. I remember your embarrassment as I dunked my head under a tap against the heat of Pompeii, and your perfect compassion as you tried to offer some of your drinking water to a heat-stricken pigeon sheltering in the ruins. I remember you, a better swimmer than I, showing me how to lie back on the floating rope that demarcated the swimming area in Vietri as though it was a hammock. I remember sipping limoncello under the lemon groves of Amalfi, and trying not to vomit on the boat that took us there. I remember having to look up the Italian word for 'niece' on my phone as I tried to explain to a waiter in Naples why I was drinking Lacryma Christi, the Tears of Christ, with you.

But I remember most clearly the conversations we had on the balcony late at night, though I couldn't repeat a single word. Trust someone older than you when he says that you won't meet many people who inhabit a world as deep and as rich as yours is. I used to be sixteen. I remember what it's like. That hunger for the world that comes with the dawning realization of how little you've seen. Everything starts to open up. You question what you've been told and long to discover everything for yourself. And you're wide open, ready to receive the world as though it's brand new. I hope that as you grow older you can hold onto at least some of that. I hope I can.

And when one day I'm swept away, vanished into the last long night as firmly and finally as the dead of Pompeii, I hope you will remember me on the balcony, with the concrete giving back the day's heat to the shimmering stars above, a wine glass lifted to my lips and a smile on my sunburned face.

The Toy Shop: Naples and the Beauty of Decay

Chi non crede all'amore non crede in Dio

Who does not believe in love does not believe in God

- WWII era graffiti in Naples bomb shelter

I wouldn't tell you the name of the street if I knew it. You have to find it. Every writer and con artist knows that you need to let people earn it. Make them do half the work, and they'll convince themselves.

It's tucked away in the warren of narrow alleys that make up this most ancient of cities. An area where bags are clutched tight and tourists are scarce. The black flagstones are worn smooth by the steps of generations of Neapolitans, and scooters and cars weave and muscle their way through gesticulating pedestrians with noisy good humor. Another anarchic corner of this anarchic city, already founded when Rome was a malarial swamp. The soft volcanic rock beneath the city is bored through with tunnels made by Greeks, and by Romans, enlarged by medieval water carriers and converted into bomb shelters during World War II. Any place that has lived so long and so brightly will have its dark corners. Naples is a city of secrets. Martyred Christians and 1940s partisans have each left their marks on the lightless walls. Under the city streets, there's a darkness that has gone unchallenged since the founding of the world. They say Dracula is buried in Naples. It's almost certainly not true. But if it was, I wouldn't be surprised.

But nothing is brighter than the narrow strip of sky between the tall buildings in the lower part of town. Nothing is more vibrant than the cries of the citizens, exchanging staccato dialect from the street below to the windows above. No city I've seen is more alive than this.

I don't remember how we first found this place, back when I used to smoke. The trade in cigarettes goes on right on the street, the prices displayed out in the open. Two euros a pack, when they're five in the store. Ten in Canada. When you live off gambling and freelance writing, every euro matters.

"Giorno, bella!" After a few visits, the seller got to know us. Neither Neapolitan nor African, the other major group in this part of town. Two smiling fools who spoke next to no Italian and were willing to brave the less photogenic parts of the city to save three euros per pack. We bought by the carton. We never figured out if the cigarettes were stolen or counterfeit. Sometimes, a man would ride up on a scooter and sell a pack or two to the store. The packs came from all over the world, judging by the languages of the health warnings printed on them. Russian script mingled with Arabic and French and English. Because we bought in bulk, we would be invited inside, into the toy shop where no toys were ever sold. She'd pour us a shot of the fiendishly strong coffee they drink in Naples and flip the top of the table that stood against one wall, revealing row after row of cigarette cartons.

Maybe it comes from living under a volcano, with the shattered top of Vesuvius looming across the glittering bay. Just to the north of the city, steam rises continuously from the sulfurous vents of the Campi Flegrei, Europe's only supervolcano. Or it could be some dim inherited memory of the relentless pattern of invasion and occupation, the bloody wars that have rolled over this city through the centuries. You could blame it on the Camorra, the vicious mafia that started in Naples back in the 17th century and still wield enormous power throughout the region and beyond. The shadow of death is everywhere here. But it takes a bright sun to cast such dark shadows. Neapolitans live as though death 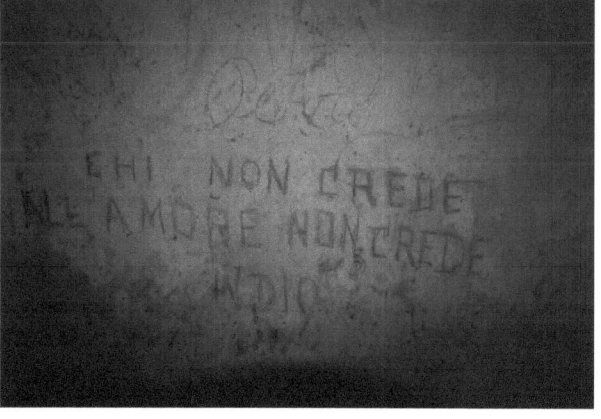 doesn't matter, as though life is forever. Viva la vita, as a woman in a bar said to me and raised her glass. This isn't a trick. And it's more than a story. They know no more than us, but the bright sun and the glowering volcano remind them each day that the world will never end. We all fall, and two more take our place. It's the immortality of weeds, the ivy that grows back thicker for being cut, that cracks marble monuments in the exuberance of its wild vitality. It's the always necessary reminder that this is a game that we play, that only comes to an end in the context of the self. Without an ego, we are infinite.

And this is how love starts. On a high hill under castle walls, we watched the whole jumbled city, pitted with church domes and skyscrapers, slide towards the sea. We rode the funicular. We wandered along the lungomare, watching stray cats emerge from the sea-scoured rocks as the sun began to sink. We tasted the best pizza on earth. We sat by the sea and listened to the fishermen singing as they steered their boats to shore, and the teenagers laughing and yelling in response, sure that the world would soon be theirs.

I don't know how many times we went to Naples. Each time we went, we discovered something else. Some new place to eat, even more delicious than the others. Some new castle or cathedral or tomb. An even more gorgeous view of the bay and the mountains and the buildings that are beautiful precisely because they are half-ruined. Because they shatter from the life that they contain, while the plastic mannequins of wealthier cities go on forever unchanged. With each visit, we fell more deeply in love with the place. You don't love a person or a place in spite of their flaws; you love them because of them.

And every time we went to Naples, we invariably saw some young couple making out. It became a sport to find them, always thinking that this would be the time it didn't happen, only to spot them in the train station or on the long walk back from the sea. For a Neapolitan, a tour guide at the Teatro San Carlo told us, passion always comes first.

*

Vedi Napoli e pui muori. See Naples and die. The city's unofficial slogan is equal parts promise and threat. To love is not necessarily to be blind. Naples has been beset with problems for almost its whole existence. Corruption and organized crime lead to the massive piles of garbage that offend the sensibilities of visiting foreigners. The area around Piazza Garibaldi, where most visitors form their first impressions of the city, feels more like Mogadishu than any part of Italy. The city has made colossal efforts to deal with its problems in the last few decades, but in Naples, poverty and crime and depredation run deep. You can see them even now, while you sip Campari in a fancy bar on the Via Toledo. It's always been this way. All of Italy's wealth is concentrated in the north, around the industrial and financial cities of Milan and Turin. And while Naples gets its share of tourists, it can't compete with the Italian bucket list superstars. Rome, Florence, and the unstoppable juggernaut of Venice, which gets 27 million foreign visitors a year compared to Naples' 7 million. And this is not a slight on those cities, each of which is heartbreakingly beautiful in its own way. But Florence is a plastic Italian Disneyland, a place for wealthy Chinese tourists to purchase designer handbags. Venice is every bit as beautiful as you hope, but it has long since ceased to be an Italian city, occupied instead by ever-growing hordes of foreign visitors. This is not the place to get into the rights and wrongs of globalization. It's global inequality and accidents of birth that allowed me to live in Italy in the first place.

But Naples still feels like Naples. It still has the gritty air of a place where people live and work and love and die. You can still see local families strolling along the seafront on a Sunday afternoon. It's still rare to find English spoken beyond the most basic level. That makes the city troublesome for lots of foreign visitors. But for those like me, it makes it perfect. Yes, there's crime. There's squalor. There's danger for those who don't take responsibility for themselves, who would rather see the world become a playground for  the wealthy. Naples defies the trend towards the unreal, the Instagram-ready panoramas of yet another fake location. Neapolitans are too busy living to care what you think of them. You're welcome in their city, but don't expect it to change.

Some people don't like the way the old buildings crumble and fall into ruin.

Some people are afraid of the street hustlers and the indifferent police.

Some people can't stand the sight of the garbage piled up during a sanitation strike.

But some people will see the beauty in the cracks. Some people want to visit a living city, where nothing works and everything glows. Some people don't begrudge the desperate a living and can tolerate the presence of the poor in their midst, knowing it's only the most arbitrary of chances that separates them.

Those people may come to love Naples like we do.

*

Naples' main tourist attraction is a chapel built by a grief-stricken madman who commissioned a sculpture of a dead body so eerily real, he was accused of turning people to stone. In the basement of the chapel, he did the next best thing, taking real cadavers and stripping away the flesh to map the circulatory system in beeswax and scarlet thread, the bright webbing spreading over the skeletons of two anonymous people that have spent their afterlife being gawked at by the likes of me. It used to be three. In the 1990s, someone stole the fetus that used to complete the creepy triumvirate of man, woman, and child.

Naples is full of strangeness like this.

But that's not what you'll take away from this city, if you ever visit. You won't forget the empty eye sockets of the glass-prisoned skeletons staring back at you, but you'll remember with more clarity the young lovers kissing on the steps at Piazza Plebiscito. You'll remember the sun, and the sea, and the food. Food that's remarkable even for Italy, and a fraction of the price you'll pay in Florence or Venice. Pizza was born in Naples, and they still do it better than anyone else. Not to mention the friggitoria, or the pasticceria, or the mozzarella di bufala that Campania is famous for. Food is life, and Neapolitans know that, and they are as good at it as anywhere else on earth.

On sunny days - common in Naples - the cigarette seller carries her tank of turtles out onto the street. She let us feed them, shaking the can of foul-smelling food into their open red mouths. We didn't have sufficient Italian, or Neapolitan, to tell her that it was the last time we would be visiting. She was a criminal, undoubtedly. But she was kind to us. And many of the people of Naples were kind to us, from the tobacconist who gave me a free lighter for trying to speak Italian, to the old man who made sure we got off at the right stop to go to Pompeii. Neapolitans love their city, flaws and all, and they want you to love it too.

For us, it was love at first sight. We fell in love with Naples on our first visit, and every time we went there afterward, that love grew. A lot of people hate this city. A lot of people understand nothing. But don't try to look past its problems. They are part of Naples, just as your problems are part of you. Naples demands that you accept it as it is, not as you might wish it were. For that, we'll always love it.

Ragazzi di Nocera

It always takes a little while. When you move every six months, every new place means you have to adjust. Too early to form opinions when you first arrive. You need to wait a little while before you can begin to know how you feel about a place.

But I liked Nocera from the start. The people were friendly, but the language acted as a wall to protect me from any unwanted intimacy. The weather was rainier than you would expect south of Naples. It's a working Italian city, not some pastel painted Eat Pray Love movie set. I missed the sea, but the mountains are spectacular.

Of course, we're not on holiday. This is our life. And life, even one as charmed as this, has its demands. We can't just ignore the tedious tasks and unending chores that have to be done. So what gets ignored instead is this: the sunset. The church bells. The old women on the benches, singing together in the darkness under the trees as evening falls. The bats that swoop in and out of the streetlight's orange halo, and the cats that prowl the garbage-strewn streets.

The boys have been here since the day we arrived, of course, and long before. They play football in the school parking lot under our balcony, every night if there isn't a storm. On the seventh floor, I'm invisible to them. But I can see them, hear them, singing and yelling and laughing, playing the same games I used to play with the kids who grew up near me. I don't need to speak the language. I know the rules. The fat kid gets picked last, and the youngest has to climb to fetch the ball when someone inevitably blasts it over the fence into the fallow fields beyond, and the winner takes his turn in goal. It's not as long ago as it feels. Not nearly as long ago as that.

There were elephants here once. Or so I like to imagine. In the right kind of light, you can watch weary African soldiers who marched all the way from Spain descend the scrubby hills into the valley. Hannibal found this town waiting for him, and shattered it. Surus was Hannibal's last and favourite elephant, his single tusk a pleasing echo of the Carthaginian general's one remaining eye. I read somewhere that it's the broad nasal cavity of the elephant's skull that gave birth to the idea of the Cyclops. Like all good stories, it's probably untrue.

Nocera's football stadium, named for a Polish pope, sends out shafts of coloured light as the national anthem rings out over the town. Italia, Italia! But when Dante stayed in the castle on the hill, there was no Italy. There were only Italians, ruled over by Spain or France or Austria or a rapid succession of popes. None of this matters when you're late for an appointment or struggling to get to work. Nocera's long history is not readily apparent the way Rome's is. There are no houses here, only blocks of apartments younger than my father.

But some things outlast marble monuments. Some of the boys downstairs have been called home, but the rest still play on under the swarming street lights. Not long now. Two years; maybe less. Already sometimes, a girl or two will wait on the concrete bench under the tree. Playing football for hours will fade in importance compared to chasing girls. And there's drink and drugs too, the destructive pastimes that will descend on these young men in their insignificant town just as they did on me in mine. The last time I talked to any of my old friends was a decade ago.

One boy is called away, but another takes his place. Before Italy, before Dante, before Hannibal, the boys of Nocera laughed and bragged and argued just as they do now, just as they will when those playing now are as dead as one-tusked Surus. None of us know when we will slip silently into the running stream of time and never surface again. But while we're here, still standing, still warm, it's a pleasure to watch it flow.

Bad Luck in Berlin

I saw him get onto the train. But I didn't pay attention. Why would I? Just another stranger in a city of strangers, riding the metro for reasons that would remain to me forever opaque.

It wasn't until the doors closed and the train started moving again that he produced his badge and spoke. Other passengers began showing their tickets. I did the same. As far as I knew, I had nothing to worry about. I had bought tickets for the ride, after all. It was only as the inspector held onto my tickets while checking those of the other passengers that I started to think something was wrong.

"Sprechen Sie Englisch, bitte?" I asked in response to his comment in German. It remains a wonder to me that my German is better than my Italian, even after living in Italy for a year and spending approximately one weekend in Germany. But I studied German in high school, and the brain is so much more malleable at that age. The things we learn as children outlast everything else, like my senile grandfather thinking he was back on the farm in Ireland while he lay in an English hospital. Besides, English is so similar to German, at least at a superficial level. That doesn't mean I speak German, by any means.

"Your ticket is incorrect." He didn't look like a ticket inspector. He was a large man, with a scruffy blond beard and a wool hat pulled down over his head. He had a badge. But I learned in Paris that badges can be forged.

"It is?"

"Yes. This is only for three stops. You have traveled for ten."

"Oh. OK."

"Please step off the train."

*

I was excited to go to Berlin. It wasn't just the history, either, though of course, that was part of it. David Bowie. Nick Cave. Lou Reed. Einsturzende Neubauten. Since I was a teenager, Berlin had always seemed like one of the coolest, most fascinating cities in Europe.

But our trip got off to an inauspicious start. Our first flight, from Nice, was cancelled. We had to take a flight from Marseille the following day instead.

So far, so bad. But our plane arrived on time at Marseille airport. When we boarded, the pilot explained that there was a problem with the plane's electronics that would need to be fixed. Some time passed. An hour, in fact. Finally, the engineers showed up and couldn't find the problem. So fuck it. We took off anyway.

English is the language of the aviation industry. Maybe that explains why no one else on this flight from France to Germany seemed as concerned as us when the pilot, towards the end of the flight, announced that there was another problem in the cockpit. We wouldn't be the only English speakers on board, of course. But it might take a native speaker to read between the lines of what was being said, and what wasn't.

But they couldn't have missed the way the plane lurched as we began our descent. You learn things about yourself in moments like this. A and I said nothing to each other. I reflected that it didn't matter. Maybe we were about to die, and that wouldn't be ideal. But nothing I could say or do would change the facts. And I didn't want to panic her. If you're going to drop out of the sky like a stone and splatter all over the tarmac, you may as well do it with some dignity.

Obviously, we didn't die. As we came in to land, the runway was lit by floodlights, and fire trucks with blue lights blazing raced our plane to the runway. The airport was ready for catastrophe, but in the end, it was simply a bumpy landing. We were elated as we climbed off the plane, glad to simply be alive while our fellow passengers seemed oblivious. That was how our Berlin trip began.

*

As the train slowed into the next station, we rose to our feet. We had our suitcases with us, en route to the airport. We weren't playing the clueless tourist card; we were genuinely clueless. So we did as we were told and got off the train at the next stop, accompanied by the ticket inspector. I saw him signal from the platform, and two other people got off the train from different cars. Another large man and a woman with stars

tattooed at the corners of her eyes. None of these people looked in the least bit like government officials.

"There is a fine," said the blond man. "60 Euros."

"Ok," I said, trying to hide my annoyance at my own stupidity. When I bought the ticket, the train had been arriving. I had hurried through the process, clearly misunderstanding what I was buying. But we had a plane to catch. I retrieved my credit card from my wallet.

The man grimaced.

"Cash only," he said.

"I don't have that much cash," I said. It was a lie. But now I smelled a rat. With our suitcases in tow, we couldn't have looked more like tourists. Easy prey for a team of wily European scam artists.

"Then I will have to call the police," he said.

"Ok," I replied. A brief pause, while we stared each other down. I dare you to call them, I thought to myself. Get the Berlin police down here. See what they have to say about all this.

"I really don't want to do that," the man said, a pale smile forming on his thin lips. "Do you have enough cash to pay one fine?"

"I think we -"

"No," I said firmly, cutting A off. I was convinced we were being scammed now. What kind of ticket inspector settles for half the fine in cash? I could see the man's associates glancing at one another.

"Do you have identification?" the blond man asked.

"Of course," I said, and handed over my Canadian driver's license. Easy enough to replace if I needed to. The man grimaced again and began to write down my address.

"Canada," he said. "It is difficult. If we have to send the fine to your address."

"So what do you want to do?" I asked.

A long moment passed in silence. I could feel A's discomfort as she waited. She's a good girl at heart, a child of the peaceful Canadian suburbs where authority figures are to be trusted. But she trusts me more. She said nothing.

"OK," the man said at last. Only then did he produce a handheld device from his jacket and begin typing on it while the machine spat out a receipt. "We will send you a fine. Purchase a ticket from the machine to continue your journey."

He was a ticket inspector. It was no scam. When we got home - France, not Canada - I emailed the Berlin metro and got confirmation that the fines were valid. And I have trouble extrapolating a lesson from all this. Because in Germany, credit cards are rarely used. It's common to pay cash. But the undercover inspectors, rough-looking as they were, had all the hallmarks of scammers. Working in groups. Demanding cash. Being reluctant to call the police. I stand by my caution, even if I was wrong in this instance. When traveling, you need to keep your guard up. The world is full of crooks, and some of the worst of them carry badges.

But take your time buying your ticket from the Berlin metro machines. Because they will check. And, as we discovered when we finally returned to Canada, they will send fines across the world if they have to.

Italy and the Meaning of Life

Show a dog something that runs, and he's going to chase it. There are men who cannot see a mountain without needing to know what lies behind it. Yesterday, we booked our flight back to Canada, and all I can do with that is write it down.

I still believe in it. Somewhere above the forest in the Western wild, there is a yellowing scrap of paper with my handwriting on it. My sin, the big one, the mistake I made and wrote down and redeemed, pursued by the memory of that ribbon of cheap paper and the words tattooed across it. It's written right there on the plane ticket, hidden in the QR code and the mysterious gibberish stamped across the bottom edge. It's waiting for me, there in Vancouver. It's been waiting forever.

This is not a sentence. At least, it shouldn't be. Once, we dreamed of this return, the drizzly city between the mountains and the sea that remains, for all I've seen in this world, one of the most beautiful places I've ever lived. It's not that Vancouver is a bad place. It's not that I don't think I can be happy there, or that I haven't been happy there before. Until two years ago, the happiest days of my life were spent in the wide, orderly streets under those cloud-crowned mountains.

But that was before all this. Before the southern sun burned the hairs on my arms yellow and the skin on my forehead brown. Before the murmuring Mediterranean seeped into my blood. Before I ever really tasted a tomato or an apricot. It's not the ragazzi kicking the ball against the wall downstairs that keeps me awake at night. It's the thought that I almost reached that high and glittering prize, but my nerve failed at the end.

I would have it like this forever. The view you get from seven floors up in a town with no building taller than this. Watching the weather come in over the same volcanic hills Hannibal's elephants traversed. The noise. The relentless sun. The donkey braying from the farm across the street as the sun sits on the shoulder of Vesuvius. Who could want anything more? Delineated by habit and custom, each day here is much like the last, and the last was perfect. The sun shines every day, and ripe fruit hangs from the trees, and the boys in the car park below play the same games I played twenty years ago, and that's the only kind of immortality that interests me.

But change, growth and decay, tonic and dominant - this is the essence of all beauty. If this place hadn't taught me that much, I might never have left at all. Nowhere else I've been is alive like this. You can track the slow heartbeat of each sun-warmed stone. The towers and temples and palaces that crumble and shatter from the bright life within them, and the weeds that sprout in the ruins to shelter scurrying lizards. It wasn't until I came to Italy and lived here for a while that I learned there are different levels of life, and that there could be a place on earth that I would feel life more keenly than anywhere else. It's not a question of pleasure, although few people on earth are better at pleasure than Italians. It has more to do with the sense of time that comes from a hot sun and an ancient culture. In a landscape dotted with ruins from two millennia ago, what's the rush? It trains you to think differently. It teaches you to understand that all you are is the sum of your experiences in any given moment. Freed of past and future, all that's left is to simply exist. And in that eternal moment, there is nothing left but joy.

And I should leave all this to make money.

We are tied to Vancouver in so many ways. I still have that condo, appreciating voodoo value while it rots in the rain. We never planned to stay away this long. Our affairs are not in order. But the sun in Italy smiles, and the warm breeze whispers that I shouldn't worry, ever, because none of this means anything

anyway. The meaning of life is simply to live, and nowhere I've been in a wandering life are people better at simply living than they are in Italy.

The Eternal City

Some things, if you watch them long enough, make you start to think that you can see the true nature of everything. The ocean. An open fire. Crowds are like this too. Sit on the cool marble steps in December sunshine by the monument to Vittorio Emanuele, and you run a real risk of thinking that you've discovered something.

It's all here. Everything human is in this square, its edges softened into beauty by the ineluctable weight of time. You can travel the world and never leave your sunny spot. Two girls chatter together in German. A family squabble in weary Romanian. Two young men share a joke in Urdu before splitting up to work the crowd from one side to another, selling frail plastic poles for phones.

Every empire ends, that's Rome's most obvious lesson. As though I were in any danger of founding a dynasty. If you go a little while not hearing your own language, you can pick it out at 100 meters, even when it's the most widely spoken language on earth. For now. All empires end. The next gadget these itinerant hawkers shill might take its name from Mandarin or Hindi.

There is a busker just over there, in the shadow of the massive wedding cake monument. The type with a speaker. He's good, and has drawn a crowd. The songs are in English, but everyone can sing along. The Beatles. Bob Marley. Phil Collins. Music is our oldest language, the mother of all the rest.

You can hear it all here. You can read people's faces. There is no need to share a word in common. We all say the same things, but they sound different when we open our mouths. The busker's bass drifts across the square; the police have closed the road between the monument and the Colosseum. You feel you could love people at this distance, their hungers and smiles and the differing fashions of all the world. Just let me keep them at that distance. Don't let them come any closer than that. Get too close, and they will pull you into the swamp, where life is a wall against the encroaching sea, doomed to failure. Get too far away, and you're barking orders, posturing and preening on the balcony while the crowd roars. Where you stand determines what you see. Kids chase pigeons around here like they do anywhere else, and before there were pigeons, they chased cats. There were always cats. They are older than Rome, and they'll outlast it.

It would be nice, wouldn't it, in the sun, to be meeting someone here? Feeling the welcoming warmth in your chest while you wait, losing the endless ticking of the clock's minute hand to the blaring of the car horns and the sound of a guitar. It needn't be a lover, though that would be nice too. To raise your head at the sound of high heels rapping on the picturesque cobblestones, a smile forming as you watch her approach, surprised and delighted all over again at just how fucking good she looks. But it could just as easily be a friend, a lonely friend with a violin and an attic room. It could be that cousin you're no longer close with. It doesn't matter. The meeting is the best part. It gets worse from there.

It's a characteristic of a life like mine that's I'm always saying goodbye. People and places are seen only in passing, the edges fuzzy like the telephone poles that whizz by in the train window, their wires sloped black bars for unwritten music. And it's in the nature of goodbyes that not all will come off the way you imagine. Even fewer the way you hope. You don't get past a certain age without knowing the terror of that phone call, the one that tells you that another part of your life has slipped below the waves forever. Compared to that, this is nothing. A holiday snap. A wish-you-were-here with a cruel question mark added, aimed with the sharp edge of time's arrow at the person I will one day be. The first word I ever spoke is a mystery lost to time, like the recipe for Roman concrete. Most probably, it was mama, or some variation on that. The first word any of us learn, though, ought to be goodbye. We will need to use it again and again. A recurring theme in the symphony, a minor key chord progression we will be forced to return to again and again.

Rome can't help but be beautiful. In its decrepitude, citizens burned the statues of marble gods to make lime and repair their drafty hovels. Ruined aqueducts poured out fresh mountain water into a fetid swamp. But now the buildings founded on the ruins are ruins themselves, and therefore ancient and precious and beautiful under the bright sun. Distance makes it all ravishing, all of it, like the young couple fighting in Piazza Del Popolo under the shadow of a 4000-year-old Egyptian obelisk dragged into the present from a different world. Even the garish parade of luxury boutiques and claustrophobic souvenir stores can't rob the red walls and smooth black cobbles of their shabby charm.

There are people in this world who can't see a beautiful thing without wanting to own it. I'm not immune. To fear is to be human, and to build walls against those fears, real or not, is the most human thing of all. For every bridge, there's a border. The airports are swarming with armed police. I bought a place in Vancouver because of the way the sun looks on the mountains and the way the sea moves. I hoped, once the paperwork was signed, that I'd have a foothold at last. Something they could never take from me. But the mountains were there long before my overpriced condo. And the sea will look the same long after I'm gone. What is most precious, most beautiful, most essential to human life is that which cannot be owned. To own a thing is to slowly destroy it.

I've said goodbye to Rome again and again. I won't do it today. There's nowhere else I'd rather be with the day stretching out in front of me, empty of all but promise. A wild sea between me and the city isn't enough to make me forget. But it's precisely this, the need to leave, that fuels the beauty. It's this that keeps the heart alive. The thousand tiny injuries that make the muscle stronger. Memory is a nice place to visit, but the past is just another way of thinking about the present. Like Dante's Inferno, the way out is the way through. The beauty of Rome is the destruction, the faded glory, the radiant residue that owes nothing to shifting sands and everything to fleeing time. This, it must be said, is all beauty. That which moves and breathes and dances must die and be reborn. And only that which moves and dies is worthy of love.

The world is vanishing from us day by day. Visions of glory fade in eyes that replace themselves cell by cell with inferior copies. To the worst part of yourself, this is horror. The meaninglessness and absurdity of a transient life. The impossibility of death to the dull part of our brains that can't believe in a world without us.

Rome holds a deeper truth. The shattered monuments and ruined statues promise that a thing becomes beautiful, not because it endures, but because it changes, yet still maintains some kernel of itself. A single day that lasted forever would soon become a hell without limits. Give me the dance of falling leaves and shifting forms, while my gray ghost wanders Rome's eternal streets eternally. One more quiet story among the infinite stories of the dancing world.

Vietri, My Love

We wait and wait for those Big Moments. You know the ones I mean. We plan for them. We save for them. A cynic might say that they never arrive. Or that when they do, they will inevitably disappoint. But instead, what if we imagine that they are already here?

We never meant to travel so long. We planned a long break, six months to a year, and then we'd return to the life others had marked out for us. Six months became two years. Two years of tracking back and forth around the Mediterranean, through Italy to France and back again to Italy, fat with sunshine, freckled with joy. The idea was never to 'find ourselves,' or any other smooth-worn cliché like that. If anything, the plan was more to ignore ourselves. And to a certain degree, we succeeded in that.

Now we're leaving. Our revels now are ended. Time and caution conspire to force us back to Canada. That's okay. There are worse places to be. But knowing that we are leaving Europe has fired in us a mania to get the best out of the place, to tip the bottle all the way back.

And so, Vietri. Our closest beach, just ten minutes away by train. Followed by a flight of black stone stairs and a steep hill that once hummed with traffic. We know this place quite well by now. But it's different today, and it's not because we know that this may be the last time.

The kids are back at school. Most of the restaurants are closed. The season is over, and Vietri drips with the gorgeous melancholy of a seaside town out of season. Just like Formia. Just like Juan les Pins. Without the voices of children, without the monotonous music of teenagers, you can listen to the ocean. And – I swear I'm not making this up –

as the church bells howl at noon, the clouds begin to part and the rough wind turns the sky a pale ceramic blue. It's been a good day.

It's been a good day, and the pastis I brought from France agrees with the foaming waves and the wake of the Salerno ferry and the purple flowers growing wild on the cliffs above the beach. You want the last time you see something you love to be special. It is.

But a moment's thought or a passing rain cloud will tell you the truth. The beauty of the experience, created by a thousand co-conspirators of time and health and luck and weather, cannot be preserved. If it could, it wouldn't be beauty anymore. We love the crashing wave for its movement, its vigour, its inevitable destruction. We welcome the sun that chases the clouds away, but a motionless sun bolted to the sky would soon become an implacable enemy. It's precisely the changing forms, the bloom and the decay, that give this coastal village its charm. Our trip, the long adventure that I know already is going to feature in memory as a lifetime high, becomes more beautiful, not less, in the fact of its ending.

And in that long light, everything turns to gold.

If you could bottle it and sell it, there would be nothing to sell. The ecstasy, the rapture, doesn't defy its own extinction; it embraces it. Trying to manufacture a moment of majesty is a sure way to prevent one. Every Christmas, every birthday, every wedding you attend will tell you the same thing. And the way the sun moves across the water, the delicate dance of sea and cloud, will only confirm what you already knew. Putting up bars around beauty, to try and hold onto it for yourself, will kill what you loved, in it and in yourself.

But the beauty is there, whether you see it or not. It's an easy thing to say, sprawled in the sunshine on the Amalfi coast. But it's there in the red ring of a pigeon's eye, or the purple feathers of its neck that catch that same sun. It's there in the rain that speckled our umbrella this morning, that's only the sea coming back to itself. It's there in a personified universe where the tiles groan with heat on the dome of Vietri's pretty little church.

It's our last time in Vietri, maybe. But the past is just a story you tell yourself over and over. And the future is a fantasy, a dream of triumph or horror that recedes even as you reach for it. It all collapses in time, the pretty churches and the frowning castles, the busts of the Emperor, the billboards and skyscrapers. There is no last time for any of this, just as the final note of a symphony is not the end of music. It's only the idea that we stand apart from the universe that makes us look for first and last, for meaning, for lessons.

The big moment you've been planning for, the one you cling to, the one you sacrificed for over and over again is the one you're living in now. Reading this. The present moment is all you'll ever have. And more than that: the present moment in which you live is all you are. A wave that breaks at the shore. There's nothing more than this. And there doesn't need to be. All rapture, ecstasy and bliss live now, and here, forever. That's Vietri.

Fake Flowers, or Lonely Without Me

I've been here before, of course. Except I was somebody else. Everywhere we go, we leave trace elements of ourselves, desquamated skin cells and the oils from our fingertips. I trace my hands along old walls as I pass, hoping to merge my little tributary with the tide of history. In 2001, I vowed to return. In 2014, I thought I'd never be back. Now, three years later, I'm here again, trying to look for the last time on the most beautiful city in the world.

But this doesn't feel like goodbye. I was somebody else when I first came to Rome, and among streets crowded with ghosts, I catch only faint glimpses of the teenager I was then. The world was different then, too. No smartphones. No Google Maps. No soldiers holding assault rifles in the public squares. I bought beer with lira and wrestled with folding paper maps and felt like an entirely different person.

Dante was just a little older than I am now back in 1300. The middle years of his life coincided with what many at the time believed to be the middle year of the world's existence. We can forgive him his shaky grasp of facts; it's not often any of us get to draw a direct line between ourselves and history. When the first plane vanished into the smoking steel structure of the World Trade Center, I was staring slack-jawed with wonder at the open eye in the centre of the Pantheon's concrete dome. The world hasn't been the same since.

I changed with it. I dropped out of university. I stopped

shaving. I used to believe in all this stuff, the rays of the sun in molten gold flowing down on us sinners from high above. I visit the same churches now as I did back then, but it doesn't feel the way it used to. I've been to the Pantheon many times since then, and it's always impressive, but never quite as impressive as it was the first time. Dante was wrong. He died in his fifties, and the world's still here.

The places we've been leave traces in us, too. When they haul my bones out of the swamp in a hopefully distant future, they'll be able to read isotopes and track my stuttering progress around the world. Somewhere in this ever-thickening body is a trace of the water of a Roman fountain, still loyally pouring out clean water long after all the emperors have turned to dust. They'll also see rings of growth from Vancouver, where the towering trees cracked Coventry's concrete. But I don't feel this way about other places I've been. Maybe they're still too fresh. Or maybe I left Rome alone just long enough so that time could form a bright jewel like amber around its perfect memory. The bony finger of an ancient saint, encased in a dazzling silver reliquary. For thirteen years, I remembered and said nothing.

Remembrance loses much of its attraction when you're in the middle of living the best years of your life. It's nothing I looked for, and nothing I planned. When I first came to Rome, I was going to be an archaeologist, if the unthinkable happened and my fiction somehow failed to support me. As it happens, I actually do support myself by writing now. But none of this was predicted. I came to Rome today to say goodbye, but I'm not all that confident that this really is the end.

Leave Rome to the living and the dead. Every day, a fresh horde of visitors pour out of Termini, ready to be fleeced by swarthy men handing out fake flowers and string bracelets. Some of them will love the place just as I do. Some will have the right kind of ears to hear the same inaudible hum I do, here and nowhere else on earth, the

impersonal machinery of history grinding us all into the void. You can't leave a mark here. You're not Michelangelo, or Bernini, or Nero. You're probably a better man than Caravaggio, but not a greater one. I came here at just the right time, in 2001. Beauty had just come into my crosshairs then. I had just learned to read, and I was hungry for more art, more beauty, more of those glimpses of eternity that the world had just begun to show me. I was a fork tuned exactly to Rome's pitch, and my first inkling of aesthetic bliss, outside of the raptures of psychosis, was here, under the same glowering statues and shadowy paintings. They are still here, of course. They will still be here long after I am as dead as Augustus. I like that. It's something like the feeling people get under a starry sky, I suppose. But in Rome, it's time, not space, that dwarfs us.

It's life through glass again. The frame that makes you really look at the painting. I don't come to Rome to see the sights anymore. I come to sit in the Piazza del Popolo or the steps beside Trajan's Column, drink supermarket beer and watch the crowds pass by. Human beings, made beautiful by distance. They don't talk to me. They don't touch me. I suppose it was weird for an 18-year-old lad to go on holiday by himself. And I suppose it's weird for a married man to go to one of the world's most romantic cities alone. I care even less about that kind of thing now than I did as a teen. Another person means another voice, and then I can't hear that hum that I come to Rome to listen to. I watch the crowds until I can see the world's hidden heart. Order rises from the chaos, the desires and inclinations of competing individuals forming a harmonious whole. It's the kind of thing mathematics can describe better than poetry. But poetry gets to the universal by way of the individual, preferable to any diagram. And any minute now, the sun may finally shine. I don't want to say goodbye to Rome under cold clouds, and my hand is finally casting a shadow on the page. Too much beer makes a man verbose, and too much beauty can make him remote. There's that sun.

Was I nervous, coming to Rome alone that first time? I don't remember. It was my first time alone in a foreign country. My first time in any place where English wasn't the primary language. There'd be no shame in it if I was. And if I was, and I had such a good time, I wonder how much that factored into my decision to move to Vancouver just two years later. Rome awoke many things in me. Wanderlust. A sense of aesthetic bliss. The sweetness of solitude. You know, the longer I sit here in Piazza del Popolo, the brighter the sun shines and the clearer my love for Rome seems. Maybe it could have been anywhere. Had I gone to Oslo in 2001, which I think I remember considering, perhaps now I would be there, chasing the same ghost for reasons that would remain just as hard to explain as they are now. But that kid didn't know more than me. He certainly wasn't happier. He may have been more creative, but he was less skilled. Perhaps he was a little braver than I am now. Perhaps he was kinder. I'm pretty sure he was better looking, but that's faint praise. What he would think, if he could see me now, is irrelevant. I don't need his approval any more than he needed mine. But I do think he was alive to the world in a way that I haven't been for a long time. It's only in Rome, among this graveyard of dusty monuments that dwarf human lives without making them seem meaningless, that I have begun to recapture that experience of being alive.

The sun is brighter now, but the wind is still strong. I thought I would always be alone. I thought I would spend my life chasing beauty, la grande bellezza, and it would wrap its arms around me, sinner that I am, and rain gifts of joy down upon my grateful head. Maybe I wasn't all that far off the mark. I don't get to spend my days wandering through a kind of blissful dream, the way I suppose I thought artists do. I'm not alone. I have a wife. I own real estate. I work. It's writing, but it's work.

But one of the criteria to truly appreciate beauty is that it be rare or remote. As much as I love it, I never wanted to live in Rome. I only ever holidayed here. It's the perilous magic of an extramarital affair, the mistress a dutiful wife can never compete with. I've never sullied the city with the quotidian and the mundane. I never wander the cobbled streets with any aim beyond pleasure. It's better that way. I loved Vancouver once, but start buying groceries in a place and the magic evaporates. For that reason, I never wanted to marry. But I did. And after a decade together, I'd still rather be with her than without. I'm not much of a romantic. It's not like I couldn't survive without her. I'd survive without A, without Rome, without Vancouver, if it came to that. But only the dying want to survive. The living want to live.

And this is probably it. The sunlight is strong now, flashing in the water that pours from the stone mouths of marble lions, and this is probably where me and Rome part ways. The wide world calls to me. I'm not made to sit still, not yet. These crowds will be here tomorrow, but I won't be among them. Beauty has followed me all my life, haunting my nights, dulling my days, and even if it had started here, this isn't where it will stop. I wouldn't know what to do if it did. And perhaps, as I like to think in my more sentimental moments, it would be lonely without me.

www.ryanfrawley.com